PIVOTAL
MOMENTS
IN HISTORY

JOHANNES GUTENBERG
AND THE PRINTING PRESS

BY DIANA CHILDRESS

TWENTY-FIRST CENTURY BOOKS
MINNEAPOLIS

For Anne, Cathy, Kathy, Kekla, Kitsy, Kristi, Nancy, Traci, and Vicki

Consultant: Paul Needham, Princeton University

Primary source material in this text is printed over an antique-paper texture.

The image on the jacket and cover is the earliest known representation of a printing press. It appeared on the title page of a book printed by Jodocus Badius Ascensius in Paris in 1511. The image was reproduced as an illustration in a 1908 edition of A Short History of the English People *by J. R. Green.*

Twenty-First Century Books
A division of Lerner Publishing Group, Inc.
241 First Avenue North
Minneapolis, MN 55401 U.S.A.

Website address: www.lernerbooks.com

Library of Congress Cataloging-in-Publication Data

Childress, Diana.
　　Johannes Gutenberg and the printing press / by Diana Childress.
　　　　p.　cm. — (Pivotal moments in history)
　　Includes bibliographical references and index.
　　ISBN 978–0–8225–7520–7 (lib. bdg. : alk. paper)
　　1. Gutenberg, Johannes, 1397?–1468—Juvenile literature. 2. Printers—Germany—Biography—Juvenile literature. 3. Printing—History—Origin and antecedents—Juvenile literature. I. Title.
　　Z126.Z7C44 2008
　　686.2092—dc22 [B]　　　　　　　　　　　　　　　　　　　　2007020215

Manufactured in the United States of America
1 2 3 4 5 6 – DP – 13 12 11 10 09 08

CONTENTS

A CHAPTER ONE LATE MEDIEVAL CHILDHOOD

Adam, my scribe, if you ever undertake

To make a new copy of my Boethius or Troilus—

May the scalp under your long locks turn scurfy [flaky]

Unless you faithfully write what I have composed!

For many a day I must do your work again,

Scraping and rubbing the parchment to make corrections—

All owing to your negligence and haste!

—*Geoffrey Chaucer, "To His Scribe, Adam," CA. 1385*

From prehistoric cave art to modern text messaging, people have always found ways to connect with one another through written symbols. Several major inventions in human history—writing, the telegraph, the Internet—expanded our powers of communication. Each new discovery made it possible for more people to reach larger audiences more easily. Like stones dropped into a still lake, these inventions created widening ripples of information and knowledge.

The most dramatic of these changes before the computer age—the biggest splash—was the European invention in the mid-fifteenth century A.D. of printing with movable type. Other ways of printing were developed earlier in eastern Asia. But the technology Johannes Gutenberg designed had a greater historical impact, not only in Europe but around the world.

In Gutenberg's day, Europe was already on the brink of a new age. Exploration, scientific discoveries, and the growth of towns, industry, and commerce were changing the political and religious structure of medieval society. Gutenberg's invention arrived just in time to push Europe firmly out of the Middle Ages (the period from about 500 to 1500) and toward the modern world.

Printing with movable type spread·quickly across Europe, starting a revolution that has yet to slow down. Even as the computer age is once again changing the world, and electronic technology has largely replaced metal type and the printing press, printed matter remains a prime means of human communication. Publishers around the world are still issuing some ten thousand books a year and almost as many newspapers a day, using an estimated 130 million tons (118 metric tons) of paper annually.

IN THE HEART OF EUROPE

Johannes Gutenberg was born about 1400, a good time for a smart, curious, inventive child to start life. He was also born in the right place, right in the middle of Europe, in the proud city of Mainz, Germany. Well situated where the

Main River flows into the Rhine River, Mainz had played a
key role in the political and commercial development of
Germany since the earliest times. When the Romans conquered northern Europe in the first century A.D., they built a
fort there overlooking the Rhine, a major artery flowing 820
miles (1,320 kilometers) from Switzerland through the
Netherlands to the North Sea.

The Roman fortifications, repaired and extended, still protected Mainz in Gutenberg's day. As a boy, Johannes could climb the walls to watch riverboats arriving from points north or south or sailing into the broad Rhine from the Main River with travelers and products from eastern Germany.

In the fifteenth century, Germany was a collection of principalities (regions ruled by princes) and dukedoms of varying sizes. They were all loosely linked in a confederation known as the Holy Roman Empire. An emperor chosen by a group of

In Gutenberg's time, Mainz, Germany, was a busy riverside town, as seen in this fifteenth-century illustration.

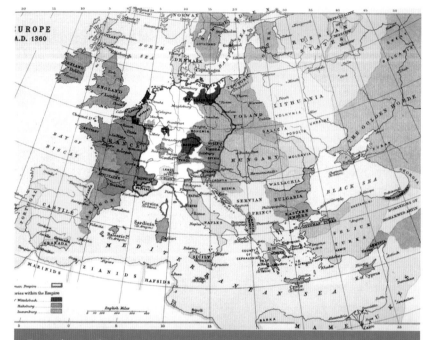

From the ninth century to the early nineteenth, the Holy Roman Empire was a powerful force in Europe. In Gutenberg's day, Germany stood at the heart of the empire. Six of the seven electors who chose the emperor were from German territories.

seven electors headed the empire. Gutenberg's hometown belonged to a large province ruled by Germany's highest-ranking Roman Catholic archbishop. Besides being an important church official, the archbishop of Mainz was also the arch-chancellor—the chief minister—of the empire and the highest ranking of the electors who chose the emperor.

GOLDEN MAINZ

The busy archbishops had little time to govern Mainz and gave that job to its most important citizens. In 1244 the archbishop granted the oldest and wealthiest families of Mainz a charter allowing them to form a town council to rule the city. Five of Johannes Gutenberg's eight great-great-grandfathers were among these Mainz patricians.

For the next century, the city grew and flourished. Mainz formed a trade alliance with other cities along the Rhine. They all agreed to a uniform currency, so that all coins minted in the various towns would have equal value. The gold gulden of the Rhineland (the region around the Rhine River) soon became the coin of choice for merchants throughout the empire and beyond.

With a pontoon bridge stretched across the Rhine at Mainz, river merchants had to transfer their goods to boats on the other side of the bridge. The ruling patricians not only collected duties but also claimed the right to purchase whatever they wished to buy before anyone else had a chance to. Mainz citizens grew rich trading in wine, lumber, grain, wrought iron, wooden furniture, and especially gold jewelry and linen and wool cloth. Hired swordsmen and lancers protected shipping from pirates.

Prosperity generated great building projects. The old Romanesque-style cathedral of St. Martin, with its sturdy walls and rounded doorways, was embellished with new additions featuring stained glass windows and pointed arches in the latest Gothic fashion. The tallest of its six red sandstone towers shot ever higher until it soared 300 feet (91 meters) above the open square. New churches and monasteries also sprang up. Before long, the spires of forty churches poked over the city walls. A new citizens' center took shape, complete with a stone market hall and a hospital. In the new city hall, town councillors in ermine-trimmed robes could lord over ordinary folk and tax them to pay for all the extravagance. Everyone called the town Golden Mainz.

GUTENBERG'S FAMILY

One of Johannes Gutenberg's great-great-grandfathers purchased all or part of a large stone house known as Hof zum Gutenberg. With two wings and three stories, the building was like a modern apartment house, large enough for several dwellings and work spaces.

In fifteenth-century Germany, the custom was to use the name of one's house as a surname. But Johannes's father, Friele, took his surname, Gensfleisch zur Laden, from other

HOF ZUM JUDENBERG?

One of Johannes Gutenberg's great-great-grandfathers purchased all or part of Hof zum Gutenberg in about 1300. Calling it Gutenberg (good mountain) was perhaps a way of hiding an older name, Judenberg (Jews' mountain), for it may have been among several properties in Mainz that had once belonged to Jewish families. In 1282, in an anti-Semitic uprising, Mainz Jews were massacred, expelled, or forced to convert to Christianity, and the archbishop took possession of their properties. Although many Jews later returned to Mainz and lived there in Gutenberg's time, the properties confiscated in 1282 remained with those who had purchased them from the archbishop.

family properties. Although the family lived in the Hof zum Gutenberg when Johannes was growing up, Gutenberg's father never used the name Gutenberg in his lifetime. Johannes's last name became Gutenberg to distinguish him from other Johanneses in the extended Gensfleisch family.

Johannes's mother, Else Wirich, was Friele Gensfleisch's second wife. Else's family did not belong to the town patricians. Her father and grandfather were shopkeepers in Mainz. They were respectable and well-to-do, but they were not members of *die alten* (the old ones), as Mainzers referred to the town's ruling class.

Johannes had an older brother and sister, Friele and Else, and also a half sister, Patze, from his father's first marriage. Patze and her husband lived at the Hof zum Gutenberg, as did other families unrelated to Johannes.

A COMPANION OF THE MINT

For a time, Johannes's father served as a town councillor, and he was also a "companion of the mint." That title meant he had some managerial role in the Mainz mint, where silver coins called groschen and gold gulden were stamped.

The companions did not mint the coins themselves. They purchased the raw materials (only patricians had the right to deal in precious metals) and ensured that each gulden had 12 ounces (340 grams) of 23-karat gold. They also hired the artisans who worked in the mint.

Johannes probably spent time at the mint learning how coins were made. Skilled metal engravers made tools called dies or punches. These were rods of steel with a pattern or a picture and lettering engraved in mirror image on one end. Other metalworkers cut and prepared blank discs of gold or silver. A third group of workers put the blanks between two engraved dies and then struck the upper die smartly with a hammer, hitting it hard enough to imprint both sides of the coin at once with the pictures and writing engraved on the two dies.

This early sixteenth-century German illustration shows workers minting coins. The worker in the center prepares the blank coins for the worker on the right who engraves the blanks with a die. The worker on the left measures each coin with calipers to regulate coin size. Gutenberg would have been exposed to the coin-minting process as a young boy.

The mint also made seals and other official jewelry for the archbishop and the town council. Johannes saw how workers melted and poured metals into molds of damp sand, wood, or metal to create large plaques or medallions with pictures and writing on them. Watching these processes, he must have noticed the relative hardness of different metals.

Johannes's uncle Johann Gensfleisch was also a companion of the mint, as were the fathers of two of his friends, Heinz Reyse and Johann Kumoff, whose families both lived in the Gutenberg house during Johannes's childhood. It is possible, as one biographer suggests, that some of these men took up the work of engraving dies and brought that work home to Hof zum Gutenberg.

A curious child would be fascinated to watch someone whittle a design into tempered steel, trimming off tiny flakes with each cut of the sharp engraving tool. Did Johannes observe such work? Did he think then that a similar process could create a means of printing words on paper?

A TURBULENT TIME

When Johannes was growing up, Mainz guldens were a respected currency, but Mainz itself was in precarious financial shape. For years the patricians, who paid few or no taxes, had been living off annual payments, or annuities, from the city. Earlier, the old families had paid the city large sums with the agreement that the city would pay them 5 percent of the total sum each year. No time limit was set on these annuities.

But after twenty years of 5-percent payments, 100 percent of the money was paid out. To continue the annual payments to patricians, the city council taxed residents who were not patricians—namely the artisans who worked hard to make the products the patricians traded, as well as the coins they used for trading.

The urban working class resented having to support the wealthy patricians. Each business had an organization to supervise training and set standards for the goods it produced or traded. These workers' organizations were called guilds. From time to time, the guilds rebelled against patrician rule. Then, in the mid and late fourteenth century, epidemics of the deadly bubonic plague devastated Europe. The population of Mainz shrank from about twenty thousand residents to about six thousand. The loss of workers helped

GUTENBERG'S BIRTH DATE?

No one knows exactly when Johannes Gutenberg was born. Considering various dates in surviving records of him and his family, scholars have narrowed the possibilities to a ten-year span, 1394 to 1404. But in the 1890s, Mainz city officials decided the turn of the century would be a good time to celebrate the five-hundredth anniversary of Gutenberg's birth. Since summer is a good time for a festival, the officials chose June 24, the Feast of Saint John the Baptist. As a result, Gutenberg's official but quite arbitrary birthday became June 24, 1400.

At its height in the fourteenth century, the bubonic plague killed almost half the population of Europe. Outbreaks continued into the sixteenth century. In this sixteenth-century German illustration, a doctor (lower center) tries to treat a plague victim.

boost the political power of the guilds, for the patricians depended on their labor to make money in trade. In fits and starts, often through riots and violence, guild members gradually gained control of the city council.

Johannes grew up during all this tension. In 1411, when he was probably approaching his teens, his father and 116 other patricians left Mainz to go live on their estates and farms outside the town. By living there, they could avoid paying town taxes that the guilds wanted to impose on them. The whole family may have gone with Johannes's father, perhaps to Eltville, a short distance downstream, where Johannes's mother had property.

The archbishop mediated a compromise, and the patricians returned to Mainz. But two years later, the same problems flared up and the patricians again fled town.

GOING TO SCHOOL

Nothing is known about Johannes's schooling. Children in medieval German towns generally learned their letters and numbers at home from their parents or from the priest at their parish church. Once they had mastered these basic skills, the children of artisans were apprenticed to learn a trade. The sons of wealthier guild members attended private town schools that emphasized arithmetic and business skills, while the sons of patricians received further education at grammar schools. The grammar taught there was Latin grammar, for all over Europe, Latin was the language of theology, law, medicine, philosophy, and science—of every field of knowledge scholars considered worth studying.

Perhaps Johannes attended classes at Saint Christopher's Church across from the Gutenberg house. Or perhaps he learned Latin at the cathedral school or at Saint Victor's, a monastery he later supported as a lay brother (someone who lives outside a religious society but is affiliated with it). Or maybe he went to the village school in Eltville. Wherever he went, he would have been taught the same curriculum. The grammar book that Aelius Donatus wrote more than a thousand years earlier was the established textbook for learning Latin.

HANDWRITTEN BOOKS

Johannes may not have owned the book. A handwritten book—the only kind of book that existed in Europe at the time—was expensive. Books were produced one by one in workshops called scriptoria, where scribes using quill pens

A scribe copies a book by hand in this fourteenth-century French painting.

and ink carefully copied other handwritten books. Some scribes were monks or nuns living in monasteries or convents. Other scribes worked in commercial shops that sold books to wealthy customers.

But Johannes did not need to own schoolbooks. Students learned by reciting their lessons aloud and by writing information in notebooks. When the class finished learning Donatus's lessons, Johannes would have a written copy for himself—in his own handwriting. Memorizing and copying are good methods for mastering information. An intelligent student who wanted to learn more on his own, however, must have been terribly frustrated by the scarcity and high cost of books.

Johannes's parents no doubt had some books at home. Many patricians owned a prayer book or a psalter (the Book of Psalms from the Bible with some added prayers and hymns) and a book of medical advice in Latin. They might also have some stories of knights and ladies and books of history, sometimes bound together into one volume, in German. The cathedral and local monasteries had small libraries of religious literature, occasionally mixed in with works by Roman authors such as Cicero and Livy. To obtain a book, a wealthy person might borrow it from a library and hire a scribe to copy it. These handwritten books might have been neatly bound in leather-covered wooden boards or simply wrapped in paper.

Paper itself had only recently come into use in Europe. The Chinese were making paper as early as the second century B.C. After the new religion of Islam spread in the seventh and eighth centuries from Arabia eastward across Asia and westward across northern Africa, trade flourished over a vast area. Many Chinese inventions, paper among them, gradually spread westward. After reaching Islamic Spain, paper moved across Europe. Italians began producing paper and selling it throughout Europe in the late thirteenth century. Gradually, other western European countries learned the process. About 1390, shortly before Gutenberg was born, the first German paper mill opened near Nuremberg. Paper mills also opened in several regions of France.

Paper made books much cheaper to produce. Before paper became available, books in Europe were written on animal

Two workers make paper in this sixteenth-century German woodcut. Fiber pulp from old rags was added to a vat of water to create a mixture called a slurry. The papermaker scooped a thin layer of the slurry out of the vat on a rectangular wire screen. The slurry dried on the screen, forming a sheet of paper.

skins that were scraped and prepared as a writing surface. In the fifteenth century, parchment (made from the skins of sheep or goats) or vellum (a finer material made from the skin of calves or other young animals) was still being used to make fine copies of important books, such as the Bible. Paper, however, began replacing skins for a variety of manuscript books. Seeing the commercial possibilities, booksellers employed scribes to copy popular writings—not necessarily anything new but something old and respected that was sure to sell. Many book collectors, thinking that paper would not last as long, still preferred to buy parchment manuscripts. But most readers welcomed the lower price of the new writing material.

Book production rose across Europe. Still, it took scribes time to copy each book by hand, working long hours to complete two, maybe four, pages a day. "Three fingers hold the pen," a scribe complained at the end of a manuscript,

MANUSCRIPTS

The word *manuscript* is derived from the Latin phrase *manu scriptus,* meaning "written by hand." It was coined after the invention of printing, as a way to distinguish between printed and handwritten books. Once printing became widespread, *manuscript* began to be used for any document submitted for publication, even one prepared with a typewriter or laser printer.

"but the whole body toils." Worse, many errors crept into their work. Authors such as the Italian poet Petrarch denounced "the ignorance of the scribes and their indolence, which corrupts and confuses everything."

UNIVERSITY LIFE

The scarcity of reliable texts was a frequent cause of lament at the universities. Gutenberg may have experienced this problem firsthand. Some scholars think Gutenberg registered at the University of Erfurt as Johannes de Altavilla (Latin for "John of Eltville") from 1418 to 1420. The curriculum leading to the final examination had a long reading list of classical and medieval works of grammar, logic, astronomy, physics, and psychology. Some students obtained books by hiring themselves out as scribes, which also helped them earn money for their tuition, room, and board. Others only "read" books by hearing them read aloud in class.

Professors lectured from lecterns (stands to support a book or other reading materials). They often read long passages in

Latin from books that the students had no access to. Sitting on backless benches, the students scribbled madly in their notebooks. Questions and class discussions were not then part of the classroom experience.

Yet it was an exciting time to be at Erfurt. The powerful Roman Catholic Church faced a growing challenge—the demand for religious reform. The church faced criticism for corrupt practices and for suppressing new ideas in science

This fifteenth-century illustration shows a professor lecturing from a lectern at the University of Paris. Multiple copies of books were not available to students, who had to take lengthy notes during class time.

This image of Erfurt is from the Nuremberg Chronicle. The fifteenth-century German chronicle used text and illustrations to recount Bible lore and stories of European people, places, and events.

and philosophy. It had recently executed Jan Hus, a Czech religious reformer, for heresy (going against church teachings). His followers in Bohemia and Moravia (the modern Czech Republic) rebelled against the church and the Holy Roman Empire. Some professors from the University of Prague came to Erfurt to escape the violence that resulted from the rebellion. These professors brought the reform issues with them, and Erfurt's faculty members were caught up in great debates. One of the most important issues was whether the Bible should be translated from scholarly Latin into common languages people spoke and understood.

The faculty often disagreed on political issues as well.

THE FIRST UNIVERSITIES IN EUROPE

The first European universities grew out of cathedral schools and monasteries during the twelfth and thirteenth centuries. The earliest universities were established in Bologna, Italy (in about 1119); Paris, France (in about 1150); and Oxford, England (in about 1167). Many more soon developed across Italy, France, and Spain. The first German universities were founded in the fourteenth century. Prague (in the modern-day Czech Republic) came first in 1348. Vienna (in modern-day Austria) followed in 1365, then Heidelberg (1386), Cologne (1388), Erfurt (1389), and Leipzig (1409). More followed during Gutenberg's lifetime and after. Mainz established a university in 1477, shortly after Gutenberg's death.

Some supported the German emperor and others the pope (the head of the Catholic Church) in their constant struggle for control over power and money. Students heard a variety of opinions that reflected those of the different religious orders the faculty belonged to, such as the Benedictines, Carthusians, Franciscans, Dominicans, Augustinians, and Brethren of the Common Life.

COMING OF AGE IN MAINZ

Gutenberg's father died in the fall of 1419, perhaps while Gutenberg was still away in Erfurt. University records show that "Johannes de Altavilla" graduated from Erfurt at the end of the winter semester in early 1420. A university education usually led to a career in the church or in government. Gutenberg was apparently not interested in either. His knowledge of books and Latin, combined with a keen interest in metallurgy and technology, would lead him down a quite different path.

The earliest document that definitely refers to Johannes Gutenberg concerns the settlement of his father's estate in

WHO WAS
JOHANNES DE ALTAVILLA?

The argument that "Johannes de Altavilla" is the same person as Johannes Gutenberg is based on circumstantial evidence. His mother owned property in Eltville. Eltville is a logical place for the family to have gone when they left Mainz as it is nearby and also on the Rhine, making it easy to reach by boat. It is possible that Johannes and some of the family remained in Eltville after peace was restored in Mainz. Although Erfurt is 140 miles (225 km) northeast of Mainz—a good three days' journey by horseback—the university was under the jurisdiction of the archbishop of Mainz. Two of Gutenberg's cousins and many other Mainzers studied there. If Gutenberg was born about 1400, he was the right age for the university in 1418–1420. Finally, searches of Eltville records have turned up no one else named Johannes of the right age to be a student in 1418.

1420. Since a legal guardian was not named for him in the document, Johannes clearly was by then considered an adult. The document also shows that he was back in Mainz. A bright, well-to-do young man, perhaps a university graduate, he was off to a good start. But it was an uncertain time. The patricians, and Mainz itself, were less prosperous and secure than they had once been. Besides, Gutenberg was a younger son in a world where firstborn boys such as his brother Friele were given better chances at success. Even Friele, however, could not inherit his father's position at the mint because their mother's father had owned a shop. Only full-blooded patricians could hold such high office—the guilds had not succeeded in changing that. Gutenberg was at a crossroads, no doubt pondering what he was going to do with his life.

CHAPTER TWO

MAN OF MYSTERY: GUTENBERG IN STRASBOURG

Witness 15. Item. Hanns Dünne the goldsmith
said, that about three years ago he earned from
Gutenberg approximately [one] hundred gulden,
solely [for] what pertained to printing.

—Strasbourg trial of 1439

After his father died in 1419, Johannes Gutenberg
remained for a time in Mainz, but political unrest continued
to plague the city. At some point, perhaps in 1428 during
one of the many conflicts with the guild members,
Gutenberg left his hometown. Historians know this because
in 1430, when the archbishop restored peace, Gutenberg
was among several patricians given permission to return.

Some patricians did return and adjusted to the political

changes. Johannes's older brother, Friele, became involved in Mainz politics, serving as one of the city's three deputy mayors. One biographer suggests that the brothers differed politically. Perhaps Friele supported the guild members' tax reforms and was willing to work with the council, while Johannes was more conservative. But political strife may not have been Gutenberg's only motive for leaving Mainz and for staying away. He was still young—probably in his late twenties—

No portraits of Gutenberg painted during his life exist. Artists working long after his death had to imagine what Gutenberg looked like. This fifteenth-century portrait shows him as a young man.

and no doubt ambitious. Quite likely he was also restless, and a larger, more prosperous city beckoned—the city of Strasbourg, a two-day journey upriver from Mainz, where documents show Gutenberg was living in 1434.

"CITY ON THE ROADS"

Gutenberg may have chosen to move to Strasbourg in part because he had relatives there on his mother's side and his family had money invested there. When Gutenberg's mother

Medieval Strasbourg was a center for trade and commerce. Riverboats and canal barges moved goods in, around, and out of the city.

died in 1433, Gutenberg apparently received as his share of her estate an annuity from the city of Strasbourg as well as several other annuities paid by the city of Mainz.

He had no reason to remain in Mainz. His two older siblings, who were both married, had inherited the family real estate. Friele retired from politics and moved to the family's house in nearby Eltville, while Gutenberg's sister Else and her husband took possession of the Hof zum Gutenberg.

Like Mainz, Strasbourg was well located for trade. The city was built on an island in the Ill River near the border of French and German lands and along the trade routes between Italy and northern Europe. Strasbourg was, as its name signifies in German, a "city on the roads." Canals crisscrossed the town, and the waterways linked the town to the Rhine, only 2 miles (3 km) away.

Strasbourg offered many advantages over Mainz. Because Strasbourg guild members had gained control of their city council earlier, residents did not suffer the intermittent rioting and mayhem that disrupted life in Gutenberg's hometown. And peace had brought growth. With a population of about twenty-five thousand—about four times that of Mainz—it was the fifth-largest city in the German empire. The streets had just been paved with stones. The cathedral of pink-tinged sandstone was rising rapidly, its impressive spire soon to tower 470 feet (143 m) above the square, making it one of the tallest buildings in the world at that time. The lower pinnacles of numerous other churches clustered nearby. The multistoried town hall, with its broad bands of round-paned windows, resembled a fine palace. The homes of the wealthy, a visitor commented, were "mansions . . . fit for princes."

More important for Gutenberg, Strasbourg was well known for all kinds of metalcrafts: bell making, jewelry making, and the carving of metal punches to create decorative leather bookbindings. Whether or not Gutenberg was already focused on creating movable type, he was doubtless attracted to Strasbourg by the opportunity to learn more about metallurgy.

GLIMPSES OF GUTENBERG

The first clue we have that Gutenberg moved to Strasbourg involves his clever maneuver to collect money owed him by Mainz. Overwhelmed by the municipal debt, Mainz city officials simply stopped paying the funds owed to Gutenberg (and perhaps other nonresidents as well). But early in 1434, the Mainz town clerk, Niklaus Wörstadt, visited Strasbourg. Asserting his rights, Gutenberg had the man arrested and jailed for the money Mainz owed him, 310 gulden. It was a lot of money, enough to pay a year's salary to a dozen skilled workers.

The Strasbourg council was embarrassed to have an official visitor imprisoned and urged Gutenberg to withdraw the charges. Gutenberg relented. First, however, he made Wörstadt swear to pay the money on his return to Mainz. The matter was settled quickly, and Gutenberg was paid. The affair shows Gutenberg as decisive and quick to act, yet ready to be reasonable. It also suggests his status in Strasbourg. Already in 1434, it seems, the thirty-something young man was known and respected in his adopted city.

Two court cases two years later open another, more puzzling, window on Gutenberg. One was a lawsuit brought by a patrician woman, Ellewibel zur Isernin Thüre. The woman accused Gutenberg of breaking a promise to marry her daughter, Ennelin. Perhaps she suspected him of seducing Ennelin, or perhaps she was trying to trick him into marrying Ennelin. The young bachelor of respectable income must have looked like a good catch. But whatever the relationship Gutenberg had with Ennelin and her mother—they may have simply been social acquaintances—he was apparently not interested in marriage.

Zur Isernin Thüre found a shoemaker, Claus Schott, willing to testify as a witness in the case. No record exists of what Schott said, but Gutenberg lost his temper and accused Schott of being "a miserable wretch who lives by cheating and lying."

A WANDERING SCHOLAR?

Gutenberg's biographers enjoy speculating about places Gutenberg might have visited during the years between 1429 and 1434 when his whereabouts are undocumented. This was not an age when wealthy young men made grand tours of Europe to further their education. Yet merchants and church leaders did travel widely on business, and students, mercenary soldiers, and pilgrims journeying to the shrines of saints also covered much ground.

It is possible, as one scholar suggests, that Gutenberg witnessed the church council that met from 1431 to 1448 in Basel (a city in modern-day Switzerland), about 200 miles (329 km) upriver from Mainz. There he would have heard church officials discussing the need for standardized religious texts. Another invented story has Gutenberg traveling along the Rhine to Holland and seeing books printed from carved woodblocks. But no block books survive from this period in the Netherlands.

But these voyages would have not been necessary for Gutenberg to be up to date on current ideas. Trade along the Rhine carried news and information of all kinds. If during these years Gutenberg was already mulling over ways to reproduce writing by mechanical means, he could just as well have been doing it closer to home, perhaps in Eltville or Strasbourg.

Schott promptly sued for libel. In response to this second case, the court agreed with Schott and ordered Gutenberg to pay the shoemaker the large sum of fifteen gulden in damages for this public insult.

The outcome of the first case, however, has been lost. Whether Gutenberg also had to pay Ennelin's mother is not known. Whatever the court's decision, records show that Ennelin was still single and living at home with her mother seven years later. As to Gutenberg, no evidence exists that he ever married anyone.

MYSTERIOUS BUSINESSES

Gutenberg meanwhile had settled in St. Arbogast, a village outside Strasbourg's city walls and a twenty-minute brisk walk up the river Ill. He seems to have chosen the neighborhood away from the center of town to have space and privacy for his work. He succeeded so well at securing privacy that we still don't know exactly what went on there. Perhaps it involved melting metals and he needed a large furnace, which would have been considered a fire hazard and not permitted in town.

The nature of this work is hinted at in court records of yet another, later, lawsuit, this one brought by Strasbourg citizen George Dritzehn against Gutenberg in 1439. The records, found scattered in three different handwritten documents, are not complete court transcripts. What we have are the testimonies of fifteen witnesses and the court's decision concerning the case. A story can be assembled from the bits of evidence, but it is like a jigsaw puzzle with several pieces missing. It seems that during those years between 1434 and 1438 Gutenberg was involved in three or possibly four different enterprises.

Gutenberg seems to have set up the first business soon after moving to Strasbourg. George's brother, Andreas Dritzehn, paid Gutenberg for lessons in cutting and polishing gemstones. Teaching, however, was not Gutenberg's primary occupation. In 1439 a goldsmith, Hanns Dünne, testified that about 1436 Gutenberg paid him one hundred gulden for something involved in a process referred to as "trucken." The key word, *trucken*, is not explained. It is often translated as "printing" but may also mean some other use of a press.

Whatever was being done, Gutenberg was probably paying Dünne for metal of some kind. Because he was neither a Strasbourg citizen nor a guild member, Gutenberg could not purchase metals wholesale. Gutenberg was perhaps making jewelry or some other decorations with gems and pressed or stamped metal. Such metalwork embellished fine bookbindings, church chalices, and jeweled boxes, called reliquaries, that held holy relics, such as a saint's tooth or a splinter of Christ's cross.

Jeweled reliquaries, such as the one shown above, were valued religious items in the Middle Ages.

PILGRIMAGES

The shrines of saints were major tourist attractions in the fifteenth century. Not everybody could afford a pilgrimage, but a surprising number of people, rich and poor alike, managed to make at least one such trip in their lifetimes.

Motives for making pilgrimages varied. Some pilgrims sought physical or spiritual healing from the miraculous powers associated with the saint. Others traveled out of thankfulness for having survived an illness or a disaster. And many just wanted to get out and enjoy the countryside and see new places.

This pilgrim badge depicts Saint Thomas Becket, a twelfth-century archbishop of Canterbury, England.

Pilgrims brought home various souvenirs of their journey, such as vials of holy water mixed with a drop of the saint's blood. Pilgrim badges, usually made of an alloy of tin and lead, advertised the places visited with images symbolic of each shrine. A palm leaf represented Jerusalem; keys, Rome; and scallop shells, Santiago de Compostela, Spain. The badges were something like modern bumper stickers from tourist attractions, only for pilgrims, these souvenirs had sacred significance.

PILGRIM MIRRORS

In 1438 Gutenberg branched out into a new venture. Taking on Hans Riffe as a financial partner, he planned to make small metal badges with convex (outwardly curved) mirrors to sell to pilgrims going to a popular shrine in Aachen, 160 miles (256 km) northwest of Strasbourg. Pilgrims purchased mirrors because they believed mirrors could trap the healing power of holy relics displayed at the shrines of saints. Convex mirrors were considered especially effective since the curved surface reflected a broad panorama.

Aachen was then the most famous shrine in Germany. Charlemagne, the founder of the Holy Roman Empire, had been buried there in 814. After Charlemagne was made a saint in 1165, a collection of other relics joined the golden casket with his remains. What many people believed were the Christ-child's swaddling clothes, the loincloth of the crucified Christ, and the Virgin Mary's dress were among the awe-inspiring objects on display. Such crowds flocked to Aachen that church officials arranged a special outdoor display for two weeks every seven years. Thousands of pilgrims surged into the open area around the church, hoping to catch sight of the holy relics draped from a gallery between the towers of Aachen's cathedral. They held up mirrors to absorb the beneficial rays for friends and relatives back home.

Gutenberg knew that metal badges with convex mirrors would sell like hotcakes. The going price for mirrors on the last seven-yearly pilgrimage had been half a gulden each. If he could turn out several thousand of these souvenirs, he could make a lot of money.

This sixteenth-century painting shows the cathedral in Aachen, Germany, and the surrounding streets. First constructed in 786, the cathedral is the oldest in northern Europe and was a destination for religious pilgrims.

The enterprise attracted two workers, Andreas Dritzehn (Gutenberg's pupil) and Andreas Heilman. They each agreed to put eighty gulden into the partnership. Both men were part of Strasbourg's new aristocracy—artisans whose families had become political leaders when the guilds gained control of the city council. The men apparently set to work, only to discover that owing to an outbreak of plague, the pilgrimage for the summer of 1439 would be postponed until 1440. They would have to wait two whole years to reap the profits of their work.

THE "ART AND ENTERPRISE"

At some point that fall, Dritzehn and Heilman discovered that Gutenberg was carrying out some work at St. Arbogast that he was keeping hidden from them. Perhaps suspecting that the money they had put into making pilgrim badges was being used for the secret project, they wanted to know more about it. The result was a whole new contract: Gutenberg agreed to take them on as partners and show them what he was doing if they would each increase their investments to five hundred gulden. Whatever this costly project was, it looked promising to the two men. Hans Riffe, his principal investor, also increased his contribution, and the men settled on a five-year contract to work on the new venture. They agreed that if one of them died, his heirs would receive only one hundred gulden at the end of the five years. All the partners were careful not to say too much about what they were doing: the enterprise was to remain a closely guarded secret.

As the project got under way that fall, friends and neighbors were abuzz with speculation about what was going on. Dritzehn's neighbor Barbara quizzed him about why he worked so late at night. A farmer who tilled Dritzehn's land wanted to know why he suddenly wanted some farm produce sold in a hurry—what kind of business was he involved in anyway? Dritzehn told the farmer he was making mirrors. But was that true?

More people became involved in the secret as the project went on. Gutenberg hired Konrad Saspach, a carpenter, to build a heavy press to Gutenberg's specifications and install it at Dritzehn's house in town. But Saspach was apparently not told how the press was to be used. Or perhaps he just knew better than to mention it later when he spoke as a witness at the trial.

Dritzehn's friends were concerned about his involvement in the mysterious business. He was borrowing from everyone, even his friend Reimbolt's housekeeper. Reimbolt himself had pawned a valuable ring of Dritzehn's for him. Dritzehn was having so much difficulty putting together the five hundred gulden that he had not yet signed the contract even though he was hard at work on the project.

Already weak with overwork and anxiety, Dritzehn fell ill at a friend's house the day after Christmas, 1438. That very day, a religious procession passed through the streets of Strasbourg chanting prayers to save the city from plague. But it was too late for Dritzehn. He was already infected. Aware that he was about to die, he told his friend about the partnership and his debts. A priest came to hear his last confession. The next day, he was dead.

When news of Dritzehn's death reached Gutenberg, his first concern was to keep the project secret. He sent his servant Lorenz Beildeck to Andreas's brother, Claus Dritzehn, asking him to take apart certain pieces of equipment "so that thereafter no one could see or understand anything." Andreas Heilman also sent the carpenter Saspach on a similar errand. But both Claus and the carpenter found that the pieces had disappeared. Did Gutenberg himself race in from St. Arbogast and risk catching the plague to be certain the item was dismantled? Or did Andreas's other brother, George Dritzehn, steal it before the others got there?

DRITZEHN VS. GUTENBERG, 1439

Andreas Dritzehn's brothers George and Claus were furious about Andreas's debts. They demanded that Gutenberg pay them Andreas's share in the venture, and when Gutenberg refused, they asked to be admitted into the partnership. Perhaps Gutenberg did not trust them, or they lacked Andreas's skills. Whatever the reason, he again refused, and that is when George Dritzehn sued him in court.

The Council of Strasbourg decided in Gutenberg's favor. Even though Andreas Dritzehn had not signed the contract, the judge argued, it was clear from his actions that he had joined the partnership. It was equally clear that the contract specified a five-year investment. In the event of the death of a partner, all the equipment and products of the business would remain with the other partners. His heirs would receive only one hundred gulden at the end of the five years. Because Andreas had not yet paid all the money needed to join the partnership—the reason he had not yet signed the contract—the judge ruled that what he still owed should be subtracted from the one hundred gulden due his heirs.

Andreas still owed Gutenberg eighty-five gulden. His brothers George and Claus hence received only fifteen gulden, no more than Gutenberg had had to pay two years earlier for insulting the shoemaker.

Even more important to Gutenberg, he had also succeeded in keeping his secret. The "art and enterprise" (as the judge referred to it in his decision) remained unnamed. All we know from reading the trial documents is that Gutenberg was working on something new and very costly, requiring a heavy investment of time and equipment. Two skilled artisans were ready to risk their inheritance for it, and it promised to make a great deal of money. After the trial, he still had two partners, his work space, and what he had learned so far. If, in the fear of his secret being revealed, he had destroyed some of the evidence of what he was doing, he could start again. He no doubt did.

LEAVING STRASBOURG

Gutenberg remained in Strasbourg for several more years, but no evidence survives of what he was doing. He must have sold the pilgrim mirrors in 1440 and used the profits to finance his secret project. In 1441 his credit was good enough for him to guarantee a loan made to a Strasbourg knight by the church of St. Thomas. By November 1442, however, he applied for a loan from the same church. Yet he was not destitute, as he paid interest on the loan in a timely manner for many years. He also regularly paid his taxes.

In late 1443, marauding bands of mercenaries (hired soldiers), out of work due to a lull in the Hundred Years War (1337–1453) between France and England, were plundering towns in the Rhineland. Strasbourg geared up for defense. Gutenberg appears on two lists that year, one of nobles and patricians required to supply horses to defend the city and the other of men to be deployed in case of an attack. These lists reveal a little more about his financial and professional status. Gutenberg's name appears among the patricians who were assessed one-half a horse. These men had assets valued at somewhere between four hundred and eight hundred gulden. Hence, Gutenberg was not very rich, but he was still well off. On the other list, he is grouped with men affiliated with the goldsmiths' guild, which suggests he was still involved in metalwork of some kind.

On March 12, 1444, Gutenberg paid his wine tax in Strasbourg for the last time. For the next four and a half years, no record survives of where Gutenberg was or what he was doing. Did he leave Strasbourg to escape the expected attack? Was he dodging the military draft? Or did he leave because the five-year partnership had expired? Did he travel to other places, or did he simply return to Mainz (where records reveal he was on October 17, 1448)? No one knows for sure.

CHAPTER THREE

THE INVENTION OF PRINTING

He took sticky clay and cut it in characters as thin as the edge of a seal. Each character formed as it were a single type. He baked them in the fire to make them hard. He had previously prepared an iron plate . . . with a mixture of pine resin, wax, and paper ashes. When he wished to print, he took an iron frame and set it on the iron plate. In this he placed the type, set close together. When the frame was full, the whole made one solid block of type.

—*Shen Kua, eleventh-century Chinese statesman,
describing the work of his contemporary Pi Sheng*

Ever since 1760, when the Strasbourg documents of 1439 were first published, scholars have argued over what "art and enterprise" Gutenberg was hiding. Many believe that Gutenberg was making small metal letters that could be arranged to form words and sentences and used to print whole pages at a time, something no one in Europe had yet done. According to this theory, the metalwork was carried out in St. Arbogast, since furnaces made to melt metal were banned as fire hazards inside the Strasbourg city walls. Metal or wooden frames holding the assembled letters would then be brought into town, where Andreas Dritzehn could test them on the press installed in his house. The four pieces—the ones witnesses at the trial said Gutenberg wanted disassembled—were parts of either the mold he was using to make the letters or the frame that held letters in place for printing a page.

If Gutenberg was experimenting with movable type, the work must have been frustrating. No printed books survive that can with certainty be dated to the years Gutenberg lived in Strasbourg. A few fragments of paper and vellum with printing were considered so worthless a decade or two later that bookbinders used them to pad wooden book covers. Found later, they provide tantalizing hints of Gutenberg's earliest successes. But even these scraps, most scholars say, were printed after Gutenberg left Strasbourg.

Is it possible the invention took him more than a decade to perfect? What took so long? The modern world takes printing so much for granted that it is hard to imagine the steps required to invent the process. With his knowledge of punch cutting, coin striking, and casting molten metal in molds, Gutenberg had a good head start. But stamping individual letters on metal or leather was still a long way from mechanically reproducing full-length pages in the elegant angular handwriting used by fifteenth-century scribes.

PRINTING IN EASTERN ASIA

China developed a method of printing centuries before Gutenberg was born. As early as the seventh century,

In this scroll from the Diamond Sutra, *printed in 868, Buddha talks to a disciple. A copy of the* Diamond Sutra, *found sealed in a cave in China in the early twentieth century, is the oldest known printed book in the world.*

Chinese artisans were engraving images and texts on wood blocks or copper plates and printing them on paper or textiles. Among the oldest examples of Asian printing are four brief Buddhist passages printed on slips of paper for the Empress Shotoku of Japan in the 760s. The world's earliest surviving printed book for which the date is known is a copy of the *Diamond Sutra*, a compilation of Buddhist teachings block printed on seven sheets of paper and glued together into a scroll 16 feet (5 m) long. A colophon (a note printed at the end) states that Wang Jie had the scroll "reverently made for universal distribution . . . on behalf of his two parents" on May 11, 868.

BLOCK PRINTING

To make copies of artwork or a written passage, Chinese artisans first smoothed a block of wood the size of the paper. They spread the surface with a thin rice paste and glued the original to be copied face down on the prepared block. Then, using special curved knives, they cut into the wood, leaving the inked lines and digging away the blank areas of the paper. When finished, the block showed the picture and the writing sticking up from the wood, only in reverse.

To print from the carved woodblock, artisans dipped a brush in ink and daubed the wood with it. They spread a clean sheet of paper on top and gently but firmly pressed the front of the paper evenly against the ink. Then they peeled the imprinted paper carefully off the block and hung it to dry. The original piece was destroyed in the process, but thousands of copies could be made from a single woodblock.

This modern painting shows Pi Sheng, an eleventh-century Chinese printer. Pi Sheng used the idea of wood-block printing to create movable type. But the clay Pi Sheng used to make his type was too fragile for repeated use.

Block printing flourished in China during the Song dynasty (960–1279), when the National Academy issued hundreds of books. The books included the writings of Confucius and commentaries on them, histories of all the dynasties of China, literary anthologies, and dictionaries. The thousands of woodblocks used to print these books were stored in huge, well-ventilated warehouses, making them available for reprinting whenever more copies were needed.

BLOCK PRINTING TRAVELS WEST

Like the manufacture of paper, block printing gradually spread westward from China across Asia and probably reached Europe in the late fourteenth century. One of the earliest surviving European woodblock prints with a date is a German picture of Saint Christopher from 1423. Gutenberg no doubt saw similar pictures of saints when he was growing up. He may also have played with playing cards that artisans in southern Germany and Italy produced using the same process.

The idea of creating books from block-printed pages must have occurred to European wood-carvers whether they ever saw or heard of Asian books. The earliest surviving examples of block books in Europe, however, are from the second half of the fifteenth century. By then Gutenberg had come up with a different process.

MOVABLE TYPE

Gutenberg probably did not pursue the idea of block printing as a way to produce books. He was not a woodworker, and the large amount of copper needed for a book printed from copper plates would be prohibitively expensive. If he was going to use metal, he wanted components he could break down and reuse, something smaller than a page. Words,

This fifteenth-century illustrated Bible is called the Biblia pauperum (paupers' Bible). Meant for poor, uneducated people, it used pictures of saints to tell biblical stories.

DID PRINTING IN ASIA INFLUENCE GUTENBERG?

Most scholars argue that travel and trade between Asia and Europe was too limited for Gutenberg to have gained much technical knowledge about printing from Asian sources. European travelers who went to China during the thirteenth and fourteenth centuries when Mongol rulers encouraged trade never mentioned printed books when writing about their experiences. Marco Polo and others noticed paper money but did not describe how it was printed. Even in the unlikely event someone showed him Chinese books, Gutenberg would not have learned anything more about printing techniques than he would looking at a playing card or saint's picture printed by a German block printer.

perhaps. Or better yet, individual letters. If he could make individual letters that could be arranged to print one page and then disassembled and reset to print another, he would have a less expensive and more flexible way to print books. This method is called printing with movable type.

The Chinese had also thought of this solution. In the mid-eleventh century Pi Sheng, "a man of the common people," devised a method of making movable type from baked clay. Each piece of type printed one Chinese character. To print a page of writing, Pi Sheng arranged the type in a frame lined with a waxy mixture that hardened to hold the type in place while printing. He then could melt the wax and remove the type for reuse.

Pi Sheng's ceramic type was apparently something of a novelty, a "precious possession" of his heirs. But it did not replace block printing. Nor did movable type made of tin, which, Chinese printers discovered, did not hold ink well and deteriorated too quickly. A third attempt, undertaken in the early fourteenth century, used movable type carved from wood to print some official records. Its inventor, Wang Chen, had artisans work for two years making "sixty thousand type or more." He even figured out how to keep track of the many different characters needed to print in Chinese. The compositor (typesetter) sat between two round tables that turned on pedestals like lazy Susans. Both tabletops, each 7 feet (about 2 m) in diameter, were divided into compartments where characters were arranged according to rhyme.

As a page printed with wooden type does not look any different from one printed with a wooden block, it is difficult to know how widely Wang Chen's invention spread. His description of the process makes clear, however, that it had not yet caught on in 1313.

Koreans also made movable type, and about the time Gutenberg was born, King Taejong established a foundry to make bronze type for printing books. The people responded enthusiastically to the effort. "There will be no book left unprinted," said one report, "and no man who does not learn. Literature and religion will make daily progress, and the cause of morality must gain enormously." When bronze ran low, people donated vases, bells, and instruments to melt down for type.

These pieces of Korean bronze type date to the early fifteenth century. The Koreans may have been the first to create moveable type cast in metal.

But making movable type from metal was costly for the Koreans, as the Chinese and Japanese found when they later adopted the process. That was because all three languages used characters representing syllables or whole words for printing, not alphabetic characters that represent individual sounds. Imagine the number of pieces of type English would need if each piece of type carried not a letter but a syllable. According to one linguistics professor, English has more than fifteen thousand different syllables. In China, Korea, and Japan, printing with movable type required thousands of characters and cost so much that only government sponsorship made it possible. As a result, much printing was still carried out with wood blocks.

THE ALPHABET ADVANTAGE

The influence of Chinese writing was so strong that no one in Asia seems to have thought of the advantages of alphabetic writing. The number of different types needed is sharply reduced when printing is based on individual sounds, not on syllables or words. To print a book in English with movable type, a printer needs only fifty-two different letters (an uppercase and a lowercase for each letter of our alphabet), ten numerals (0 to 9), and perhaps thirty other symbols and punctuation marks. That adds up to fewer than one hundred sorts of type. Of course, the printer needs many identical copies of each letter and symbol to compose each page for printing. The number increases quickly if a printer also wants to use italics, boldface, or different sizes of type. But the total still remains well below the thousands of different pieces of type needed for Chinese.

GUTENBERG'S CHALLENGES

Working without the benefit of knowing how printers in eastern Asia produced movable type and fixed it in a frame for printing, Gutenberg had a number of steps to master. No one knows the exact procedures Gutenberg followed in developing his invention. Based on the printing he produced and later evidence of how printing was done, scholars have analyzed the problems he faced and suggested how he solved them.

First Gutenberg had to decide how to make the type.

GREAT SCRIPT

One Korean king did see the usefulness of alphabetic writing. In 1446 King Sejong introduced a whole new system of writing Korean based on the individual sounds of the language. He called it "the correct sounds for the instruction of the people." He hoped that since it was easier to learn and better represented the sounds of the language than Chinese characters, more of his subjects would learn to read. Printers, however, did not make use of these individual letters for type. They continued to use whole words.

The educated classes opposed the new writing, and a later king banned it in the early sixteenth century. During the late nineteenth century, Korean nationalists revived the alphabet and named it *Hangeul* or Great Script. *Hangeul* remains the official writing system of both North Korea and South Korea. But children still learn many Chinese characters, which are occasionally used in academic papers and official documents.

With his knowledge of metals, he probably did not even think of modeling pieces of type from clay or carving them from wood. One possibility would be simply to carve each individual piece of type from metal, just as punch cutters cut dies for minting coins or for tooling leather. But cutting one punch can take a skilled worker a full day, and Gutenberg needed thousands of pieces of type to work with. Just setting one page of the Bible—and it is possible that printing the

Bible was in his mind from the start—would take 2,600 pieces of type. He wanted a quick, easy way to produce type. By carving a punch or die for each letter or symbol, he could use it to make a matrix—a mold from which a relief (raised from the surface) design can be made. The matrix could then be used to make many identical letters. He may also have cut punches with individual pen strokes instead of whole letters and used several in combination to make matrices for each letter.

Next, he had to work out how to make the mold. The mold had to produce not just the raised image of a reversed letter but also a metal stem or body to hold the letter. The dimensions of each piece of type had to be very precise. First, the height of the body had to be exactly the same for every piece of type so that the printing surface would be flat. Otherwise, only letters that stuck up higher would get printed, leaving blank spaces where shorter letters did not touch the page being printed. Second, the baseline of the letter on the typeface had to be the same as that of all other pieces of type so that the lines of print would be straight and not dance up and down on the page. The width of each piece of type, however, had to vary, since some letters, such as *i*, are narrow and others, such as *m*, are wide.

Until recently, scholars believed that Gutenberg designed an ingenious adjustable mold that made every piece of type the exact height and depth required. By using two L-shaped pieces that slid together, the width could be easily adjusted. The matrix slipped into the base of the mold for the body of the type. By changing the matrix, the same mold could be used for any letter. Finally, all the metal parts

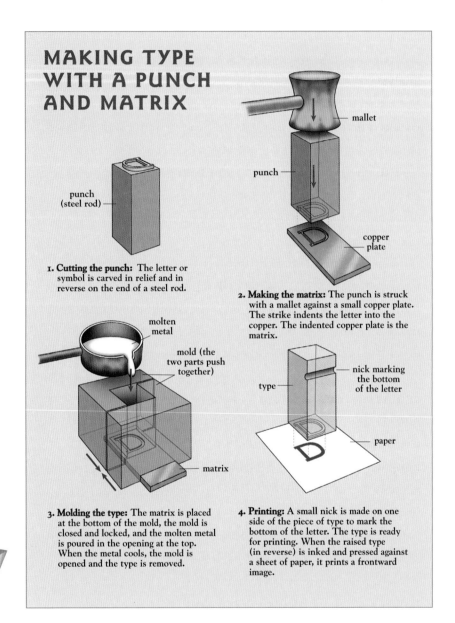

MAKING TYPE WITH A PUNCH AND MATRIX

mallet

punch

copper plate

punch (steel rod)

1. Cutting the punch: The letter or symbol is carved in relief and in reverse on the end of a steel rod.

2. Making the matrix: The punch is struck with a mallet against a small copper plate. The strike indents the letter into the copper. The indented copper plate is the matrix.

molten metal

mold (the two parts push together)

nick marking the bottom of the letter

type

matrix

paper

3. Molding the type: The matrix is placed at the bottom of the mold, the mold is closed and locked, and the molten metal is poured in the opening at the top. When the metal cools, the mold is opened and the type is removed.

4. Printing: A small nick is made on one side of the piece of type to mark the bottom of the letter. The type is ready for printing. When the raised type (in reverse) is inked and pressed against a sheet of paper, it prints a frontward image.

of the mold were encased in wood. That way, the worker casting the type could hold the mold steady with one hand while pouring the scalding metal with the other.

In recent years, however, two scholars at Princeton

University challenged this assumption. Using a computer to analyze a papal bull (a letter or decree from the pope) printed by Gutenberg in 1456, they noticed many unusual variations in letters. This suggested that all the pieces of type used for a particular letter were not produced with one matrix. They concluded that these letters were cast in temporary molds made of clay or sand. If so, the adjustable mold was a later invention.

MORE CHALLENGES

As important as creating a mold was coming up with the right combination of metals to pour into it. Gutenberg needed an alloy that would melt easily, yet would harden quickly. It could not be very expensive—he needed too many pieces of type. He was familiar with mixtures of lead and tin from making pilgrim badges, and perhaps he had already discovered the usefulness of antimony when creating the convex mirrors. Lead and tin shrink when cooling from a liquid to a solid. Antimony, on the other hand, expands as it cools. Since the dimensions of each piece of type had to be exactly right, Gutenberg wanted an alloy that would not shrink or expand but harden to the perfect size. By trial and error, he came up with a formula that historians estimate was about 83 percent lead, 9 percent tin, 6 percent antimony, and 1 percent each copper and iron.

Once he had produced a set of type and made plenty of copies, especially of frequently used letters, he had to compose them into lines of text and lock them firmly in place for printing. For this he used a wooden frame that probably opened on one side so that the compositor, or typesetter, could slide each line into place as he finished it. Slivers of wood slipped between the type and the frame acted as shims to hold the type tight.

It was a major breakthrough. At last, Gutenberg had the equivalent of a woodblock to print from. Only this block, called a form, was made of durable metal and its components could be easily disassembled and rearranged to print something different. A few thousand pieces of type could print hundreds of copies of many books.

The next problem Gutenberg faced was finding the right ink. Water-based ink used for block printing did not spread evenly on the metal typefaces. Again, no doubt by trial and error, Gutenberg came up with a mixture that seems to have included lampblack (soot scraped from glass placed above a burning candle and used as black pigment in water-based inks), heated lead and copper oxide, and boiled oil, possibly linseed oil. The idea may have come from artists' oil paints, which were just coming into use. Probably owing to the unusual, high metallic content of his ink, the texts he printed with this ink remain an impressive deep, glossy black to this day. No one knows the recipe for this ink.

To spread the ink, Gutenberg may also have invented the ink balls that became standard equipment for printers. These mushroom-shaped tools are hemispheres about the diameter of softballs. They are made of leather stuffed with wool or hair and attached to wooden handles. With an ink ball in each hand, the inker rubbed the ink balls first in a tray of ink and then rolled them across the lines of type with just enough pressure to spread the sticky ink evenly.

Gutenberg's most memorable innovation was devising a printing press. He may have tried first to print by rubbing sheets of paper against the inked type, as woodblock printers did. If so, it took a lot of time and hard rubbing to get the ink to penetrate the paper or parchment, and it would have been hard to press evenly on every part of the page. But maybe he thought of a press right off. Presses were not unusual items. They were used in a number of industries. Winemakers' presses extracted juice from grapes. Papermakers' presses squeezed the water out of paper.

In this fifteenth-century painting, workers use a press to squeeze juice from freshly picked grapes. As the workers turned the upright wooden screw (center), the horizontal arm put pressure on a container of grapes. Gutenberg adapted this technology to print ink on paper.

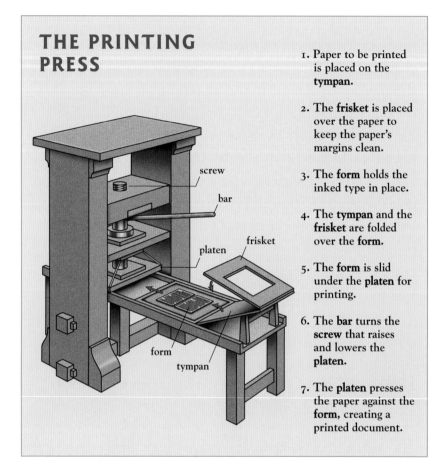

THE PRINTING PRESS

1. Paper to be printed is placed on the **tympan.**

2. The **frisket** is placed over the paper to keep the paper's margins clean.

3. The **form** holds the inked type in place.

4. The **tympan** and the **frisket** are folded over the **form.**

5. The **form** is slid under the **platen** for printing.

6. The **bar** turns the **screw** that raises and lowers the **platen.**

7. The **platen** presses the paper against the **form,** creating a printed document.

Labels in figure: screw, bar, platen, frisket, form, tympan

Bookbinders' presses held gatherings of pages firmly in place for sewing. Gutenberg was already doing something that involved a press when he paid the Strasbourg gold-smith Hanns Dünne one hundred gulden in 1436. (Many scholars use the word *printing* in translating Dünne's testi-mony, but no evidence exists that Gutenberg was already using a press to print at that time.)

Although Gutenberg did not invent the press, he was the first to use one for printing. And he designed that press, again most likely by trial and error, to get the results he wanted. He did it so well that printers made no basic changes in the design for more than three centuries.

WHEN AND WHERE DID GUTENBERG BEGIN PRINTING?

The questions remain: How long did all these inventions take? When and where did Gutenberg develop this art? Some scholars suggest that all the mystery in Strasbourg concerned some new technology for making pilgrim badges or mirrors faster and more cheaply than his competitors. The process somehow involved a press and molds that he did not want anyone to see. Others argue that he was already printing while he was in Strasbourg.

Some biographers look at the time gap between March 1444 (the last time he paid taxes in Strasbourg) and October 1448 (when he took out a loan in Mainz) and speculate about where Gutenberg was for those years. One story puts him in Avignon, France, where a Czech named Procopius Waldvogel was offering to teach "the art of artificial writing" using letters of iron, tin, brass, and lead. At one time, some people were willing to believe a sixteenth-century legend that printing with movable type was invented in Haarlem, Holland, in 1440 by Laurens Janszoon Coster and that Gutenberg went there, worked for him, and stole his ideas.

The real story will probably never come to light. Too many records have been lost. But it is not just time that has obscured Gutenberg's story. Gutenberg himself surely contributed to it. Secrecy was paramount. He could not let too many people know what he was doing.

GUTENBERG'S MYRIAD INVENTIONS

In developing the process of printing with movable type, Gutenberg is credited with:

- Creating separate pieces of metal type for every letter and symbol, either by carving a punch for each one, using the punches to make a matrix for each one, and using the matrices in a mold to cast many individual pieces of type, or by some other method

- Devising an alloy of lead, tin, and antimony to make type

- Designing a mold, perhaps one that would hold a matrix and adjust to different letter widths

- Designing a compositor's stick to assemble each line of type by placing individual pieces of type in the correct order, which was then transferred to a frame for printing

- Designing a frame to hold the type in place for printing

- Finding the best formula for ink to use on metal letters: an oil-based ink using lampblack and oxides of lead and copper

- Making inking balls to apply ink to the type

- Designing a press with a platen (flat metal plate) to press the paper or vellum evenly against the inked type and a screw to lower and raise the platen to apply and release the pressure.

In a time without patents to protect inventions, he could not be too cautious. Europe was in dire need of a good method for duplicating books and other forms of written communications. Many other inventors were tinkering with a variety of ideas about how to do this. Gutenberg was the first one who had the persistence, the determination, maybe even the obsession—as well as the talent—to succeed.

CHAPTER FOUR

THE RETURN TO MAINZ

All that has been written to me about that marvelous man seen at Frankfurt is true. I have not seen complete Bibles but only a number of quires [several sheets of paper folded in half, one inside the other] of various books of the Bible. The script was very neat and legible, not at all difficult to follow—your grace would be able to read it without effort, and indeed without glasses.

—Aeneas Sylvius Piccolomini, in a letter to Cardinal Juan de Carvajal, March 1455

Records show that Gutenberg was back in Mainz in 1448. Perhaps he returned to make it easier to collect the annuities the town owed him. Or perhaps he was looking to tap new sources of money by talking friends and relatives there into investing in his projects. If so, it worked. In October a cousin, Arnold Gelthus, borrowed 150 gulden on Gutenberg's behalf. Gutenberg agreed to pay 5 percent interest on the loan each year.

He probably also had another reason to return to Mainz. His sister Else died sometime after 1443, and Gutenberg quite likely inherited the family house. Here he would have plenty of space for a workshop, and he and his assistants could live there as well. This opportunity more than made up for Mainz's continuing financial and political problems. Not only would all that space be rent free, but having the entire operation in one place would make it easier to keep what was going on secret from prying eyes and nosy neighbors.

DK TYPE

How much Gutenberg brought with him from Strasbourg can only be guessed at, since historians disagree as to how far along he was in creating all the inventions that culminated in printing. But whatever he had learned came with him. He would have brought any tools he had completed—typecasting mold, compositor's sticks, printing frames, and inking balls. The press itself would be easy enough to rebuild. Several assistants, including the carpenter Konrad Saspach (who left Strasbourg around that time), may have accompanied him to Mainz.

The first type Gutenberg designed and used for printing came to be called DK type. The font is based on a thick, rectangular handwriting called textura, used in Europe for the most formal type of writing. The letters are narrow, with straight, angular lines instead of curves. The parallel upright strokes are evenly spaced, giving the writing the appearance of a loosely woven textile of thick black threads.

The height of the lowercase letters is about 0.3 inches (0.8 cm), a relatively large type. It is the equivalent of about 22 points in modern printing terms. A type that large is not efficient for printing lengthy books, but it is very readable from a distance or in poor light. It would be useful in a book to be read from a lectern.

EARLY PRINTING PROJECTS

Once enough type was cast and the various steps developed, Gutenberg was at last ready to go public with his invention. His first publishing ventures were small projects that gave him a chance to perfect the printing process and to work out the logistics of running a print shop.

One of the oldest surviving fragments of printing attributed to Gutenberg is a scrap of paper the size of a postcard printed with DK type, front and back, with eleven lines from a popular 750-line German poem, *The Sibylline Prophecies*. In it a sibyl, or prophetess, reveals the future to King Solomon, telling him about the life of Jesus and the later history of the Christian church. The poem strongly criticizes corrupt popes.

Perhaps to save on paper, Gutenberg set the poem like prose, so that the entire poem would have filled about twenty-eight pages. The print on the surviving fragment is poorly aligned. Some letters are dark, others barely visible. Obviously, Gutenberg was still working out how to cast type of an even height. Years later, a bookbinder thought so little of this badly printed book that he cut up a copy to use as scrap paper. He used the surviving piece to line the wooden covers of a better-printed book.

DK type, however, was not made for printing *The Sibylline Prophecies*. It lacked several capital letters, such as *K*, *W*, and *Z*, that are common in German. Undoubtedly, the type was designed for printing Latin. Gutenberg knew well that works in Latin would sell all across Europe. Printing the grammar book from which he learned Latin as a boy was a logical place to start. The *Ars Minor* of Aelius Donatus was the most widely distributed book of the fifteenth century—the perfect project for creating a steady cash flow for Gutenberg's new business.

Tightly laid out, Donatus's text took up only twenty-eight pages. None of the copies Gutenberg printed that survive, however, are complete. Like textbooks everywhere, they probably got worn with use and finally discarded. Most of the existing fragments were found in the bindings of books in Mainz and Basel. Scholars who have carefully studied these fragments estimate that Gutenberg printed at least twenty-four different editions of the work. All of these fragments are printed on parchment or vellum, not paper, because animal skins last longer. Large quantities of parchment and vellum were not easy to come by, so print runs (the number of books printed at one time) were probably small. If Gutenberg printed two or three hundred copies of each edition, however, the total—produced over ten or more years—adds up to thousands of books.

By analyzing the condition of the type, scholars can tell that the earliest edition of Donatus preceded the printing of *The Sibylline Prophecies*. The others came later. The dates of all these editions are debatable. Those who think Gutenberg was already printing in Strasbourg put the earliest Donatus edition

Gutenberg printed this page from Aelius Donatus's Ars Minor (a Latin grammar book) about 1450.

at 1442. Those who support Mainz as the birthplace of printing suggest sometime between 1448 and 1452. Gutenberg's press continued to issue Donatus editions until 1458 or later.

JOB PRINTING

The Latin grammar texts were not the only moneymakers for Gutenberg's print shop. In the early 1450s, a new market opened for Gutenberg's invention. In 1453 Turkish forces captured the city of Constantinople, toppling the Byzantine Empire, which had long dominated southeastern Europe and

western Asia. Europe had seen it coming. In 1450 the
Mediterranean island of Cyprus, ruled by a French dynasty,
had appealed to the pope for help against a threatened
Turkish invasion. The pope authorized the sale of letters of
indulgence—religious documents that released the buyers
from penalties for their sins. The money raised would be used
to pay mercenaries for the defense of Cyprus. Thousands of
identically worded letters were needed for this fund-raising
drive. Handwritten indulgences took a long time to produce—a scribe could turn out only two a day. It was the perfect job for a printer.

This sixteenth-century Italian painting depicts the first Turkish attack
on Constantinople (modern Istanbul, Turkey) in 1453. The threat of
war in Europe meant business for Gutenberg, as the leaders of the
Roman Catholic Church sought to raise money through the sale of
printed indulgences.

LETTERS OF INDULGENCE

Letters of indulgence were a controversial means of fundraising by the Roman Catholic Church in the late Middle Ages. The letters were based on the idea, dating back to early Christian times, that a person's sins could be absolved by an appropriate penance. If a person performed good works, fasted, prayed, went on a pilgrimage, or gave to the poor or to the church, that person's sins would be forgiven and he or she would suffer less in the afterlife.

In the thirteenth century, the custom developed of giving people a kind of receipt for donations of money to causes officially sanctioned by the church. These receipts were called letters of indulgence or simply indulgences. Church agents known as pardoners sold these indulgences, which had blank spaces for the pardoner to fill in the name of the purchaser and the date of sale. The letters explained the purpose of the donation and stated that the purchaser was absolved—that is, the person would not have to undergo punishment for any sins. The purchaser was expected not just to buy the indulgence but also to go to confession and receive absolution (formal forgiveness) from a priest.

The earliest indulgence from Gutenberg's print shop that still survives is dated October 22, 1454. It is printed in Latin on one side of a piece of vellum slightly larger than half a sheet of modern printer paper. Gutenberg set only the headings and opening phrases in DK type. For the thirty-one lines of text, he created a new, smaller type of about 14 points that he modeled

Gutenberg printed this letter of indulgence in 1455. The indulgence
was sold to raise money for the defense of Cyprus.

on the handwriting of official documents. This writing, called
bastarda, has curvier lines than textura and is easier to read.

Over the next six months, until the fund drive ended in
April 1455, Gutenberg issued about seven impressions (printing without making changes or resetting the type) of this
indulgence, which were all sold in the archdiocese of Mainz.
Of the possible thousands that were printed, forty-one survive.

The Turkish threat gave Gutenberg other work as well.
At the end of 1454, he printed a political tract organized by
months like a calendar. *Eyn Mahnung der Christenheit Widder*

Die Durken—A Warning to Christendom against the Turks—screamed the title of this six-page pamphlet.

Using DK type again for German, the *Türkenkalender*, or Turks' Calendar, appeals, month by month, to various European leaders—the pope, the emperor, and several monarchs, princes, dukes, and city officials—urging them to take arms against the Turks. The December segment celebrates the news of a successful defeat of Turkish forces at the border of Hungary—news that reached Germany in early December 1454. The tract was apparently printed in time for holiday gift giving, as the text ends with the first known printed New Year's greeting: *"Eyn gut selig nuwe Jar"*—A happy, blessed New Year!

All of these smaller jobs were what the Germans call bread titles. They provided income for food and supplies. Gutenberg's assistants could do much of the work involved. That gave the inventor time to devote his creative energy to a larger project, one that required a far larger capital investment than the indulgences, pamphlets, and twenty-eight-page booklets he was producing. For Gutenberg was eager to make his mark in a big way. He had in mind a real book, an impressive tome of many pages, an elegantly printed book that could compete with the finest manuscripts.

A NEW FINANCIAL PARTNER

Soon after Gutenberg returned to Mainz, set up his printing business, and began selling copies of Donatus's grammar book to schools, he found a kindred spirit ready to invest large sums in his dream. This was someone he could trust to

(JOHANNES GUTENBERG AND THE PRINTING PRESS)

Eighteenth-century French artist Jean-Antoine Laurent painted this study of Gutenberg working in his print shop.

keep the technical details of his new invention secret.

Johann Fust, like Gutenberg, was a metalworker. He had accumulated some wealth as a merchant, however, and it seems at least some of his wares were books. It may be that he was helping sell the grammar books, taking copies to Frankfurt and other cities where he traded. Johann Fust's brother Jakob, also a metalworker, was a member of the Mainz City Council. Like the Dritzehn brothers, the Fusts were members of that newly rich class of guild members who were edging out the old aristocracy in Germany.

About 1450 Fust lent Gutenberg eight hundred gulden to purchase equipment for a new print shop to be devoted entirely to the new project. Within a short time, it became clear that even eight hundred gulden would not be enough for what Gutenberg had in mind, and Fust made a second loan of eight hundred gulden. Gutenberg said later that Fust promised not to insist on the 6 percent interest written into the contract, but both men agreed that if Gutenberg could not repay the loan when the project was complete that Fust would own all the equipment Gutenberg purchased with the money. Gutenberg then had enough support to carry out his dream project.

A WORTHY PROJECT

In 1451 a German cardinal, Nicholas of Cusa, was traveling throughout Germany and Austria as a papal legate (a representative of the pope) urging church reform. One of the issues he stressed was the need for churches and monasteries to have accurate copies of the Bible.

Gutenberg knew that monasteries under pressure to buy a Bible would be grateful to pay less for a printed one—provided it was accurate and looked as good as a handwritten Bible. Here was the challenge Gutenberg was looking for.

Historians do not know the exact manuscript Gutenberg followed in planning his printed version of the Bible. The Library of Congress has a manuscript Bible called the Great Bible of Mainz that is very similar in text and layout. Gutenberg must have purchased or borrowed such a Bible from a monastery or church in Mainz and taken it apart to use as a model.

The manuscript Gutenberg followed in printing his first Bible may have resembled this one, the Great Bible of Mainz.

The new shop was probably set up in a different location. One possible place for it was the Humbrechthof, a large unoccupied house that belonged to a Gutenberg relative. New presses were built for the shop, and new workers were hired and trained in the new technology. The men already working for Gutenberg probably helped. Although he belonged to the goldsmith's guild, Fust does not seem to have been involved as a craftsman on the project.

Gutenberg designed a new textura type, slightly smaller than DK type, and set to work casting it. The new type included many more variants of letters and more ligatures (type with two or more letters) than the DK type. Instead of the 202 characters of DK type, Gutenberg and his workers produced 290 assorted pieces of type. The new type was still large enough—about 20 points—for someone standing at a lectern or a pulpit to read aloud to a congregation.

Huge orders for paper and vellum were sent out. The paper was ordered from Italy and carted over the Alps and down the Rhine to Mainz. Securing enough vellum must have been tricky, as the industry was geared to supplying

THE BIBLE IN
THE MIDDLE AGES

The Bible used in the Middle Ages was the version Saint Jerome translated in the late fourth and early fifth centuries into Latin from the original Hebrew, Aramaic, and Greek languages of the Old and New Testaments. Saint Jerome also wrote introductions to each book. Over the centuries, copyists made many changes to this *Biblia Latina* (the Latin Bible, also known as the Vulgate). Frequent efforts were made to standardize the text. The last major overhaul had been at the University of Paris in the thirteenth century.

Most people did not own Bibles and not only because they were expensive. The church did not encourage laypeople to read the Bible on their own and forbade translations into vernacular languages—the languages, such as German, that people spoke every day. Theologians studied and wrote about the Bible, and priests interpreted its lessons for their parishioners. Monks and nuns made copies of the Latin Bible. These handwritten books, beautifully decorated and bound, were displayed and read from in churches. And in every monastery and convent, a monk or priest read the Bible aloud during meals.

scriptoria, not printing presses. The time it took to raise calves and prepare the skins could not be sped up.

PRINTING THE BIBLE

No one knows exactly when work began. Maybe Gutenberg started casting type about 1450, when the first money came in. How long it took to make enough type to begin printing is not known. The printing perhaps got under way about 1452. At first, four teams worked simultaneously on four presses. Each team had one compositor with a type case full enough to set at least three pages—7,500 to 8,000 pieces of type. In this way, while the compositor set one page, a second page could be printed and a third page disassembled. The manuscript they worked from was divided into four parts so that each compositor had pages to follow as he filled his stick and slid each line into the form.

Two printers manned each press. One inked the type in the form, and the other placed damp paper or vellum on the tympan, carefully aligning it with to holes made as a guide. He then folded the frisket over the paper and finally folded the frisket and tympan together onto the inked type. Next, this type-ink-paper sandwich was slid under the platen. The printer pulled the lever to lower the platen so that it pressed the ink evenly into the paper. The platen was then raised, the form pulled back out and opened, and the printed paper removed and hung to dry. Plenty of space was needed to hang sheet after sheet as the printing progressed.

Many workers assisted each team. Paper came the right size for printing, but someone needed to cut the prepared

This twentieth-century painting shows Gutenberg's print shop in full swing. Printers, inkers, and other workers concentrate on their tasks, as Gutenberg (center right) *checks a printed page.*

calfskins. Then both paper and vellum sheets had to be pricked with a needle to mark the area for printing. Someone was busy dipping sheets of paper or vellum into a bath of water and placing the wet sheets among dry ones in a stack so that the dampness could seep into all the sheets. Someone else was wiping off the ink, taking apart the forms once enough copies were printed, and redistributing the type into its type case. When the ink had set, another worker took the printed pages and stacked them in proper order. Order was important because each sheet of paper or vellum went into the press four times, until two pages appeared on each side. Once all four pages were printed and dry, someone folded the sheet and assembled it with others into quires.

GETTING THE PAGE SEQUENCE RIGHT

Gutenberg's Bible was what is called a folio, which means that each sheet of paper or vellum was folded once. Five folded sheets were tucked together to make a quire. Since each sheet was printed with four pages (two on each side), each quire comprised twenty pages. This structure had to be taken into account when printing each sheet.

Gutenberg is believed to have printed each page in order. The first page had to appear on the right half of a sheet of paper or vellum. The second page was printed on the back of the first page, on the left-hand side of the turned-over sheet. Across from that second page (on the right side of the sheet), however, came, not the third page, but the nineteenth, and on the back of that page (to the left of the first page) came the twentieth.

Just take pieces of paper, fold them in half, and assemble them into a booklet. Then number the pages in your booklet. Take it apart and see where the numbers are on each sheet. Easy. But you can imagine how tricky it must have been for the assistant stacking partly printed sheets to remember what came next in the busy workshop. He had to supply the printer with a fresh sheet for the third, fifth, seventh, and ninth pages of every quire and then start bringing back partly printed sheets in reverse order until the quire was totally printed. Modern photocopy machines and computer printers keep track of details like these for us.

STOP THE PRESS!

Work began with the idea of printing every page with two columns of forty lines each. Perhaps that was how Gutenberg's manuscript model was written. But after printing about 150 copies of the first nine pages, Gutenberg had second thoughts. He adjusted the spacing between the lines and printed page ten with forty-one lines. It did not look crowded. He trimmed the type some more and squeezed in forty-two lines. He liked it. The pages still had wide margins (wider on the outside edges and on the bottom) just like manuscripts. Putting that many lines on each page was also more economical, but the savings were only about 5 percent, so it may be that he simply thought the tighter lines looked better. At any rate, forty-two it was. The presses got going again.

Gutenberg made two other decisions after printing got started. He had thought that he could print the headings at the start of each prologue and book in red ink, as they were red in manuscripts. But this would require another pass through the press, a very time-consuming process. Instead, after printing a few, he left the spaces blank so that a rubricator (literally, a red applier) could fill them in by hand later, just as was done in the scriptoria when handwritten books were produced.

Soon he decided to make a larger print run. Instead of 150 or so, he would add maybe 30 more copies. Perhaps he had been calculating the savings of printing forty-two lines on a page and, figuring out his stocks of paper and vellum, decided he had enough for more copies. At any rate, the compositors had to go back and reset those early pages. Enough copies of the Gutenberg Bible survive that scholars

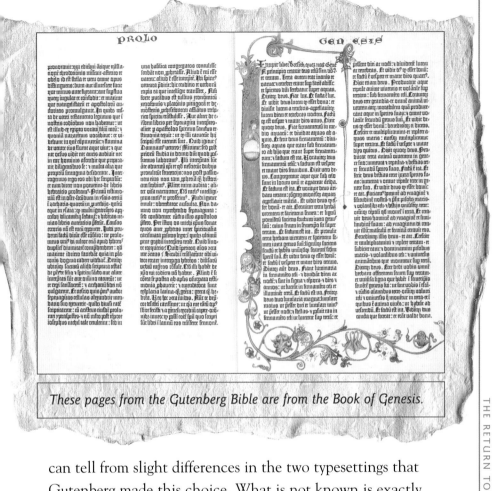

These pages from the Gutenberg Bible are from the Book of Genesis.

can tell from slight differences in the two typesettings that Gutenberg made this choice. What is not known is exactly how many copies were printed.

As work got under way, two more presses were added to the project. Perhaps it seemed like the project was taking far too long, and Gutenberg (or Fust) wanted to speed things up. Many scholars have estimated how long the whole project took. The entire Bible came to 1,282 pages (which were usually bound in two volumes). Printing 180 copies would require nearly a quarter of a million pulls on the press. At a rate of 8 to 16 pages an hour, even six teams working full time seven days a week would take about a year. But the

Gutenberg's printing office is on display at the Gutenberg Museum in Mainz, Germany.

project began with fewer than six presses, and the printers probably worked less efficiently and made more mistakes at the beginning. Also, the many religious holidays celebrated in the fifteenth century may have cut into work time. Hence, it is likely that Gutenberg and his workers spent two years seeing the Bible through the press. A scribe may have taken just as long to produce a similarly elegant handwritten copy of the same work—1 manuscript copy to Gutenberg's 180 printed copies.

A MASTERPIECE

In October 1454, Aeneas Sylvius Piccolomini, bishop of Siena, Italy, and a papal legate to the court of the Holy

Roman emperor, was in Frankfurt for a meeting of the German diet (imperial assembly). Frankfurt's annual fall fair was under way, and among the products featured at the fair were books. All the buzz that year was about a "remarkable man" with quires of a new Bible, "absolutely free from error and printed with extreme elegance," on display. The man—probably Fust, not Gutenberg—was apparently taking orders for finished copies.

Writing from the imperial court in Vienna the following March, Piccolomini apologized to his friend, the Spanish cardinal Juan de Carvajal, for not having ordered a Bible for him while he was in Frankfurt. For now, Piccolomini feared they were already sold out. "Buyers were said to be lined up even before the books were finished," he warned. Still, he promised to try to find one for the cardinal.

We do not know if the legate succeeded in securing a copy for his friend, but the Bibles certainly sold. Monasteries snapped them up. Private buyers also bought copies to donate to monasteries. The Bibles left the print shop as unbound pages, together with a list of instructions for rubricators to follow. The new owners arranged for rubricators to write in the headings and to highlight God's name and capitals at the beginning of sentences with red ink. Hired illuminators painted large decorative capital letters at the start of every chapter and whatever designs in the margins the owner desired. Binders sewed the quires together and supplied leather-covered board bindings. The lavish artwork added to many of the Bibles is a testimony to the high regard the proud owners had for the beauty of Gutenberg's printing.

The "42-line Bible," as Gutenberg's Bible is called by bibliographers, is a masterpiece of printing. Forty-eight copies survive today, twenty of them with all their printed pages intact, the ink still a deep black. Neither the paper nor the vellum has yellowed or turned brittle. The right-hand margins are justified—that was a new idea of Gutenberg's to make all the line lengths even. Only hyphens and punctuation marks occasionally push lightly into the margin as small reminders of the handwritten ancestors of this magnificent book.

THE PARTNERSHIP ENDS

Gutenberg's achievement is all the more impressive considering all the other printing he was also responsible for in the early 1450s. Perhaps the job printing at Gutenberghof did not need his constant supervision. Nevertheless, he was running two different businesses and must have been spending time at both.

Fust, however, could not have been pleased with the arrangement. He had put a lot of money into getting the Bible printed, and Gutenberg was not devoting all his time to it. The work was probably taking far longer than Fust had imagined it would, and here was Gutenberg busy getting other work done. Worse, he was not paying the interest on Fust's loan.

Sometime in 1454, things began to go sour between the two partners. Fust was perhaps having difficulties paying interest on the loan he took out to have money to invest. He must have resented the work Gutenberg was doing at his other press, including designing another type for indulgences.

Maybe Fust decided he could get in on the act. A new group of indulgences appeared early in 1455 (the earliest surviving one is dated February 27). The display lines were printed in the same type as the Bible. The text, however, was in a version of bastarda, slightly different from the one used in the earlier indulgences and based on handwriting used around Cologne. Some scholars have suggested that perhaps Peter Schöffer, one of the new hires working on the Bible, created the new type. Schöffer had trained as a calligrapher. Did Fust wangle himself a commission to produce indulgences for the area around Cologne and ask Schöffer to make this type? One of Gutenberg's biographers proposes that this was Fust's attempt to get even with Gutenberg. It is also possible that Gutenberg himself got the order to make indulgences to sell in Cologne and worked with Schöffer on the new type.

But where were these indulgences printed? Was the Bible

Gutenberg (right), Fust (center), and Schöffer (left) confer in this 1849 illustration.

already finished? It is hard to imagine that either Fust or Gutenberg would interrupt printing the Bible to turn out a thousand or so indulgences—that is, unless cash was so short that they needed money to eat.

These questions cannot be definitively answered. But the relationship between the partners deteriorated to the point that in late 1454 or early 1455, Fust sued Gutenberg for the total amount of the two loans plus the compounded interest of 6 percent—about 2,026 gulden.

It was a disaster for Gutenberg. He did not have that kind of money nor any way of raising it quickly. The Bible was either complete or nearly so and every copy spoken for, but collecting payment from the various purchasers would take time. He must have been devastated.

The court records of this suit do not survive. The only document about it was written on November 6, 1455, some six to twelve months after the original hearing of Fust's suit. The claims and counterclaims summed up in the document are complex. There was some investigation into whether all Fust's money had gone into their "common profit" or whether Gutenberg had used some of it on his other jobs. Gutenberg was asked to show all his receipts and expenditures to the court and was told he would have to reimburse, with interest, any money of Fust's not used for printing the Bible. In the end, however, the decision came down to one issue. If Fust could swear that he had borrowed money to lend to Gutenberg and had been paying interest on it, then Gutenberg had to pay him all that interest.

The hearing at which Fust was to make his oath was held November 6. Gutenberg did not attend. Perhaps hoping to delay the decision or too discouraged to face the outcome, he sent two assistants and a priest, Heinrich Günther, who had probably served as the theological consultant and proofreader on the Bible printing.

Fust was unwilling to postpone the hearing. He placed his fingers on the holy saint's relics the notary held up and swore that he had borrowed 1,550 gulden and paid yearly interest of 6 percent on that amount.

That was it. Gutenberg lost the case. Fust took over the print shop and installed Schöffer as his master printer. The two took over a new project that Gutenberg had already been working on, an even more stunning, technologically amazing printing feat—the Mainz Psalter.

It is not clear whether Gutenberg made any payment to Fust, but he apparently did lose the larger print shop and everything in it. He was not left empty-handed—he must have earned something from the indulgences and had some share of the profits earned by the Bibles. But this setback must have been hard on him. He had spent his life developing this new technology, and it had landed in the hands of his worst enemy. His carefully protected trade secrets had slipped beyond his control. What was he going to do now? Did he think of giving up?

GUTENBERG'S TYPES

Gutenberg is credited with designing or helping to design seven different types in a range of sizes and styles, all based on fifteenth-century handwriting styles.

• **DK type:** This is the first type Gutenberg developed, about 1448. It is called DK because it was first used to print Donatus's (the *D*) grammar book and several calendars (the *K*, for German *Kalender*). Based on textura script, it is also known as Blackletter or Gothic. It is about 22 points.

• **B42 type (below):** This textura type was designed for Gutenberg's first Bible, in the early 1450s. It is known as B42 because there were 42 lines in each column. It is about 20 points.

Propter quod

• **31-line indulgence type:** This type was used for printing indulgences in 1454. Based on bastarda script, it is about 14 points.

- **B36 type (below):** B36 is a DK type improved for printing the Bible, about 1459. It fits 36 lines per column.

- **Large and small psalter types:** Gutenberg is credited with contributing to the two kinds of textura type used by Peter Schöffer and Johann Fust in printing the Mainz Psalter in 1457. The psalter types are about 48 and 28 points.

- **Catholicon type:** This type was created for the reference book known as the *Catholicon*, printed in 1460. It based in part on humanistic script. It is about 12 points.

CHAPTER FIVE

THE SPREAD
OF PRINTING

On the third day of October, 1458, the king [Charles VII of France], having learned that Messire Guthemburg . . . had perfected the invention of printing with types and punches . . . ordered the chiefs of the mint to nominate some persons of proper experience in engraving . . . so that he could secretly send them . . . to obtain information about the said . . . invention . . . and to learn the art. . . . It was directed that Nicholas Jenson should make the journey, [so that] the knowledge of the art and its establishment should be achieved in this realm.

—*August Bernard, De l'origine et des débuts de l'imprimerie en Europe (The Origin and Beginning of Printing in Europe), 1853*

Gutenberg was no doubt deeply distressed to lose the business he had devoted his life to for so many years. But he was not defeated. He still had his presses and type at Gutenberghof and the loyalty of several skilled workers. He may have pocketed at least some profits from his magnificent Bible. Even more important, he lost neither his determination nor his considerable skills. Nor could Fust's actions erase Gutenberg's great achievement. Although Gutenberg's name appears nowhere in any of the Bibles he printed, word of mouth carried his reputation along the trade routes of Europe. Enough people knew he was the inventor of printing and mentioned it in writing—among them the king of France—that Gutenberg's name was not erased from history.

After 1455 the two printing houses in Mainz became separate businesses. Fust, of course, was number one. He had several advantages over Gutenberg: the six presses, Gutenberg's two new psalter types in different sizes and his design for printing large two-color capital letters, stacks of vellum scraps for smaller jobs such as indulgences, and any other supplies left over from printing the Bible. Fust also employed some skilled, experienced workers, particularly the talented young Schöffer.

In 1457 the firm of Fust and Schöffer issued one of the most beautifully printed books in the world, a collection of psalms and prayers known as the Mainz Psalter. Scholars of early printing credit Gutenberg with working out the technical difficulties for the splendid red and blue capital letters printed at

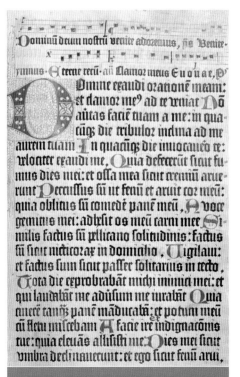

This page is taken from Fust and Schöffer's Mainz Psalter.

PRINTER'S MARKS

Printers Johann Fust and Peter Schöffer were the first to use a printer's mark, or device, placing it just below the colophon. Their mark featured two shields hanging from a curved branch, printed in red ink. Soon other printers were designing similar trademarks for their work. As title pages came to be used, printer's marks moved from the back of the book to the title page. Modern publishers often place their marks on the spine of the book as well.

Fust and Schöffer's 1457 printer's mark

the opening of each psalm. Yet at the end of the book, the printers inserted a colophon, naming only Johann Fust and Peter Schöffer as the creators of this remarkable work.

GUTENBERG MOVES ON

It is difficult to tell how severe the economic setback was for Gutenberg. In June 1457, his name appears as a witness to a sale of property. To serve as a witness, he had to possess property himself—probably Gutenberghof and maybe also the house in nearby Eltville. But the following year, he stopped paying interest on a loan he took out from the church of St. Thomas in Strasbourg in 1442. The church tried to have

Gutenberg arrested for defaulting on the loan. But it did not succeed because Mainz laws protected residents against claims from outside. Since Gutenberg had paid the interest every year until 1458, it is doubtful he was just taking advantage of the laws—he must have been hurting financially.

The ongoing output of printed matter in DK type shows he was still at work. There were Donatuses, calendars, and more indulgences, this time to raise money for missionaries. One calendar, printed in Latin about 1456, gave medical advice, indicating the best times for bloodletting or taking laxatives. It is the first known printing of a medical work. Another calendar, printed in German, listed important days of the year, such as special saints' days. A third calendar, apparently poster sized (only fragments survive), provided astronomical information for lay astrologers.

In 1456 Gutenberg also printed a papal bull in the original Latin and in a German translation. In the bull, Pope Callistus III was seeking funding for a new crusade, this one to stop the Turks who were laying siege to the Serbian city of Belgrade. Other church-related jobs included a list of all the archbishoprics (places archbishops hold power) in the world and a prayer printed as a broadside (a single large sheet of paper or parchment printed only on one side), perhaps intended to be hung up in churches.

Even though these "bread titles" kept Gutenberg and his workers from hunger, it seems unlikely that Gutenberg's ambition was satisfied with producing them. Whether or not he longed for another triumph such as the Bible or the Psalter, he must surely have wanted to get back into the business of printing books. At last, sometime in the late

1450s, Gutenberg found a new patron. Dr. Konrad Humery, the leader of the Mainz City Council, agreed to finance the cost of a new project.

PRINTING SPREADS BEYOND MAINZ

About that time, perhaps for financial reasons, Gutenberg apparently sold the DK type. By then the type was about ten years old. Over the years, many of the original pieces of type had worn out, and Gutenberg had made many improvements when he cast new ones to replace them. He also added characters to give compositors more choices in the size and shape of letters. Whoever purchased this new, improved type used it to print a Bible with thirty-six lines in each column.

Although the printer's name is not known, the neat lines of print make clear that he was an expert printer. Historians believe that this printer took Gutenberg's type and set up a printing works in or around Bamberg, a town near the Main River about 120 miles (190 km) east of Mainz. Early owners of surviving copies were located around Bamberg, and the type was next used for a book definitely printed there.

Something quite new was happening: printing was spreading. Instead of one "enterprise and art," to be kept secret at all costs, the new invention was no longer under wraps. The printer of the 36-line Bible had most likely learned his printing skills from Gutenberg. Apparently, the printer had Gutenberg's blessing to start his own shop.

WATERMARKS

Like a company logo on a label, watermarks on paper identify the mill that produced it. In the fifteenth century, most paper was made from linen rag slurries and dried in frames closely strung with wires. Papermakers at each mill stitched an identifying design in the wires that was impressed in the wet paper. Popular designs included initials, crowns, crosses, stars, animals, human figures, plants (an acorn, grape clusters, pinecones, a cloverleaf, or flowers), tools, and structures (a tower or a mill). The finished paper, held up to the light, shows the markings of the closely strung wires, called laid marks, and the mill's identifying design, called a watermark.

This grape cluster watermark was used in the Gutenberg Bible.

When manuscripts or early printed books lack a colophon, watermarks can help scholars discover where and when the book was produced. More than fifteen thousand watermarks used between 1282 and 1600 can be identified.

At about the same time as the unknown printer began printing in Bamberg, two other printers, Johann Mentelin and Heinrich Eggestein, began printing books in Strasbourg. It is quite likely that both of these men knew and worked with Gutenberg during his time in Strasbourg and that one or both went with him to Mainz for several years. By 1457 they were back in Strasbourg making their own textura-style type. In 1460 Mentelin issued a Bible with forty-nine-line columns. Eggestein began publishing Bibles a few years later.

It was like the start of an epidemic, with Gutenberg, in Mainz, the source of the infection. The workers he trained carried the new art to other towns. Some historians suggest that Gutenberg paid his workers in part with copies of works they printed. Using the skills they learned in Mainz and the 42-line Bible as a model, these Bamberg and Strasbourg printers started their own businesses.

Printing was no longer a secret, and Gutenberg was evidently encouraging its spread. Perhaps he was getting a kind of revenge on his old partner Johann Fust. But more likely, he was beginning to realize the implications of the new invention. Not only was it going to spread anyway, but it was going to change the world. He began to see that it was his mission to teach and train workers in the new art, make books widely available at a reasonable cost, improve the accuracy and reliability of books, and promote learning across Germany and Europe.

Metalworkers who heard about Gutenberg's invention came to Mainz hoping to master the techniques Gutenberg had pioneered. In 1458 King Charles VII of France ordered the director of the French mint, Nicholas Jenson, to go to

Germany to learn the craft of printing and bring it back to France. It is likely that Jenson was among the students gathered at Gutenberghof.

PUTTING INFORMATION AT SCHOLARS' FINGERTIPS

The project Gutenberg undertook next was even more ambitious than printing the Bible. Instead of another finely printed religious book produced for display in churches and monasteries,

In this fifteenth-century illustration, a subject offers a copy of his book to King Charles VII of France. Charles was very interested in bringing the art of printing to France.

Gutenberg chose something far more practical—a major reference work. The *Catholicon* that Johann Balbus, a Dominican friar from Genoa, Italy, compiled in 1286 included a Latin grammar and a very detailed dictionary. Educated clerics and laypersons consulted it for all kinds of information.

Gutenberg began again from scratch. He made a whole set of new type. For a model, he chose not the stately black letters of textura script but something more like the open, rounded, easier-to-read script that was popular in fifteenth-century Italy. Letters of the Catholicon type still have many

HUMANISTIC SCRIPT

Beginning in Italy in the fourteenth century, most of Europe experienced a rebirth of culture and scholarship known as the Renaissance. During this period, scholars called humanists rediscovered many works from ancient Rome and Greece. Often they found them in manuscripts made during an earlier period of European scholarship and learning—the Age of Charlemagne (also known as the Carolingian Renaissance) in the eighth and ninth centuries. Scribes at that time developed a very neat, clear writing known as Carolingian miniscule. Renaissance scholars adopted this script because it was beautiful and easy to read and because they associated it with the classical literature they admired. This humanistic script became the basis for modern lowercase letters and the roman types still in use.

of the decorative details of Gothic type, but it is much closer to a modern roman type.

The Catholicon type was also smaller than any type Gutenberg (or anyone else) had yet produced. The print is about 12 points, a size still widely used in books. It was small enough to fit sixty-six lines on a page and forty or more characters in each of the two columns. Without sacrificing legibility, Gutenberg squeezed a work that would fill 1,500 manuscript pages into 744 printed pages.

The layout is also focused on practicality. On most pages, no fancy oversize capital letters distract from the information. And since such a book was not intended for

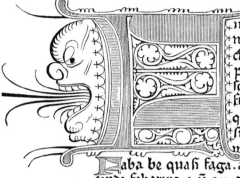

in latinis dicconibus poni
mus uti fama filius. Jn gre
ds uo dcoiiibus ph.ut or
pheus pheron. hoc tamen
scire debemus.q non tam
fixis labijs pnudanda est f
quo ph.atq B solu interest
sicut diat priscianus in pri
mo libro majoris.
aba be quasi faga.a fagin quod e comedere.
vnde fabarius a u quod fit de fabisul quod per
tinet ad fabas.et B fabarius.i.cantor et diceban
tur apud gentiles cantores fabarij.da illo legu
mine maxime urebant in cibo.et p componem

This page was taken from Gutenberg's 1460 Catholicon. The right edge of the type is left uneven, or ragged, unlike the edges of earlier printed books.

continuous reading, Gutenberg made no effort to align the right-hand edges of the columns. These are left uneven, or ragged, like text produced on a word processing program set to "flush left." Some historians consider Gutenberg's success in making such a serviceable type one of his chief contributions to the development of typography.

One scholar proposed that Gutenberg printed the *Catholicon* not with individual pieces of type but with strips of metal (called slugs by later printers) cast to print two whole lines of type at a time. The purpose of creating two-line metal plates would have been to avoid the problem of single pieces of type falling out of the form, which occasionally occurred. This method had the disadvantage that individual letters could no longer be disassembled and reassembled. For that

THE FIRST PRINTED PICTURE BOOK

While Gutenberg and his students focused mainly on providing Latin texts and tools for scholars, in the 1460s a new printer in Bamberg launched printed books into a new area. Albrecht Pfister used the B36 type to publish popular literature in German. He had the further idea of illustrating his books with woodcuts. Although his typesetting skills were not the best, the simple woodcuts appealed to readers. The earliest dated book in German and the first dated example of a book with printed text combined with woodcut illustrations is *Der Edelstein*, a collection of fables by the Swiss writer Ulrich Boner, which Pfister issued in 1461. The two hundred illustrations interspersed throughout the text were colored by hand after printing.

reason, it was useful only for books that the printer expected to reissue at a later date.

If Gutenberg did use such a process to print the *Catholicon*, then he also invented stereotyping (using a plate cast from a printing surface). The evidence for this is still under discussion in scholarly journals. Yet the idea that he was experimenting with methods of printing even after producing his masterpiece certainly fits the picture of Gutenberg as a tireless inventor—ever creative, always tinkering, improving, and trying new ways of doing things. Only that sort of person could have invented all the things he did.

THE COLOPHON

At the end of the *Catholicon*, Gutenberg printed the only colophon known to have accompanied his work. Unlike Fust and Schöffer, who include their own names as the creators of the various books they printed, Gutenberg does not mention himself.

"By the help of the most high," the colophon begins, "at whose bidding the tongues of children become eloquent, and who often reveals to the lowly what he conceals from the wise; the noble book *Catholicon*, in the year of our Lord's incarnation, 1460, in the mother city of Mainz of the renowned German nation . . . , without help of reed, stylus, or quill [the writing instruments of scribes], but by a wonderful concord, proportion and measure of punches and formes [forms] has been printed and finished."

In other words, Gutenberg said it is God who made possible the mechanical reproduction of this book. The colophon concludes with a call to praise God and pay "tribute to the Church for this book. Thanks be to God."

The flowery language is typical of the period. The biblical allusions and the religious tone have led some scholars to suggest that a priest wrote it, perhaps Heinrich Günther, the priest who assisted as a consultant and proofreader when Gutenberg's Bible was being printed. But even if Gutenberg did not write the colophon, he must have agreed with the spirit in which it was written. Printing, he seems to be saying, is not my accomplishment but a wonderful gift from God. The colophon resonates with a sense of mission. Gutenberg seems to be telling us that he prints books not to win fame and fortune but to make another divine gift, the gift of knowledge, accessible to all.

WAR INTERVENES

If Gutenberg had other large, ambitious projects in mind, events in Mainz prevented him from carrying them out. Just as struggles between guild members and patricians had affected Gutenberg's younger days, in the early 1460s, an outright war between two contenders for the seat of archbishop of Mainz disrupted any plans he might have had. The issues concerned the age-old struggle for political power between popes and emperors. Gutenberg, along with most of the citizens of Mainz, seems to have been on the side of Diether von Isenburg, the newly appointed archbishop of Mainz. Diether objected that the pope had doubled the assessment (taxes) on Diether's archdiocese. When he refused to pay the money demanded, the pope excommunicated (banned him from Catholic rituals) him. In his place, the pope appointed a new archbishop, Adolf II of Nassau, who also had a lot of support among church officials.

Princes and nobles took sides, offering troops to defend the rights of the two rival archbishops. The country, the town, and even families were split over who was right. Like campaign managers in a modern election, Fust and Schöffer kept busy printing political pamphlets and broadsides. Some of their tracts defended Adolf, while others defended Diether. It was the first propaganda war of the age of print. Gutenberg stayed out of it.

In June 1462, Diether's troops suffered a defeat in open battle and retreated behind the walls of Mainz. That fall, in a dramatic night attack, aided by traitors within the city, Adolf's forces took the town. Gutenberg was likely among the citizens herded into a town square the next morning expecting they would have to swear loyalty to Adolf. Instead, the citizens were immediately driven out of the city by armed mercenaries. They lost everything they owned, much of it to looting. Adolf annulled all the annuities being paid to the now-exiled citizens. He gave Gutenberghof as a reward to one of his supporters.

For Gutenberg, being forced into exile must have been even worse than losing Fust's lawsuit. He lost his home, his presses, and his sources of income. He managed, however, to carry out the Catholicon type. Most likely he went to Eltville. Some of his workers may have accompanied him. Gutenberg had friends and family there and

After being exiled from Mainz in 1462, Gutenberg probably moved to Eltville (shown above in a modern photograph).

possibly also property. His brother had died, but his niece still lived there, married into the patrician Bechtermünze family. By the mid-1460s, two Bechtermünze brothers had established a print shop. In 1464 they issued an indulgence, set in Catholicon type, and later a book known as *Vocabularius ex quo*, which was a revised and much abridged version of the dictionary portion of the *Catholicon*. Although the *Vocabularius* is not as well printed as the *Catholicon* and Gutenberg is not named in the colophon, he and his workers no doubt played a role in the Bechtermünze enterprise.

The archbishops' war also scattered many other workers who had trained as printers in Mainz. Ulrich Zell headed north down the Rhine to Cologne, where he began printing books for students. Berthold Ruppel went upstream to Basel. Konrad Sweynheym and Arnold Pannartz crossed the Alps and set up a print shop at a monastery in Subiaco, Italy, near Rome. Printing was on the march.

RECOGNITION

On January 17, 1465, Gutenberg received a letter from the archbishop. In it, the man who three years earlier had banished him from his home addressed him as "our dear, faithful Johannes Gutenberg."

The letter welcomed Gutenberg back to Mainz. In recognition of his "agreeable and willing service" as well as any future such service, the archbishop appointed Gutenberg as "our servant and courtier [one who attends the court of a prince or king]." Adolf left the specific service unnamed. Perhaps he was referring to the indulgence printed in Catholicon type in 1464. Or perhaps he referred more generally to the establishment of a printing works in Eltville, where the archbishop had his palace. Church officials were becoming aware of the usefulness of the press in shaping public opinion.

Adolf was busy consolidating his power by forgiving his enemies and compensating them for their losses. In this letter, he singled Gutenberg out for special treatment by elevating him to noble status. The letter stated that as a courtier he would receive clothing every year "like one of our noblemen." He would also receive twenty *malter* (more than 60 bushels, or 2,180 kilograms) of grain and two *fuder* (about 530 gallons, or 2,000 liters) of wine. All these gifts were tax free. Gutenberg was not to sell any of the grain or wine but was to use it for his household. That would include servants, workers in his business, and any extended family members that shared his house. The archbishop's generosity probably made it possible for Gutenberg to entertain many friends as well. The archbishop also guaranteed Gutenberg exemption from military service, watch duty, taxes, and any other payments levied on citizens of Mainz.

Gutenberg moved back to Mainz, perhaps dividing his time between the town and the village of Eltville. But Gutenberg did not have many years to enjoy the archbishop's beneficence. He died early in 1468, when he was in his sixties or early seventies.

The only surviving notice of Gutenberg's death is a handwritten note in the margin of a book printed some years later: "A.D. 1468 on Saint Blasius' Day [February 3] died the honored master Henne Ginsfleiss [the name by which Gutenberg was best known in Mainz] on whom God have mercy." The note seems to be accurate. On February 26, 1468, Humery wrote a letter thanking the archbishop for allowing him to reclaim the "forms and tools for printing" that he had supplied for Gutenberg to use.

The age of print was barely under way. In the fourteen years since the 42-line Bible had created such a stir in Frankfurt, printing had expanded a little each year. Already a wide variety of texts had appeared: religious texts, official documents, political leaflets, grammar and reference books, medical advice, astrological charts, and classical and popular literature. The invention mostly followed the rivers, going eastward on the Main to Bamberg, southward on the Rhine to

The page above is from a fifteenth-century illustrated German history book, Weltchronik (World Chronicle).

Aldes Manuce operated a printing press in Venice, Italy in the 1500s. The expansion of printing led to the spread of ideas throughout Europe.

Strasbourg and Basel, and northward on the same river to Cologne. It had also wandered to Augsburg in southern Germany and across the Alps to Italy, but it was still very much a German innovation. Probably only a handful of people sensed the explosion soon to occur.

CHAPTER SIX

THE PRINT REVOLUTION

We should note the force, effect, and consequences of inventions which are nowhere more conspicuous than in those three which were unknown to the ancients, namely printing, gunpowder, and the compass. For these three have changed the appearance and state of the whole world.

—*Francis Bacon*, Novum organum, Aphorism 129, *1620*

Gutenberg's invention hit Europe running and never slowed down. In the first fifty years, printing shops sprouted throughout Germany and spread northward into the Netherlands, southward into Italy, eastward into Poland, and westward into France. Printing's reach soon stretched in a giant X from southern Spain to Sweden and from Sicily to England.

Shops were established in more than 250 towns, although many of the businesses were short lived. Competition was fierce. Like the many start-ups and failures of dot-com companies in the 1990s, the new technology attracted more entrepreneurs than could possibly succeed. Even though later printers did not have to pay for a long period of trial and error, as Gutenberg had to do, the initial investment was huge.

In the year 1500, perhaps as many as two thousand different editions of books, pamphlets, and broadsides were produced in more than seventy European towns. Printers also produced calendars, charts, proclamations, and advertisements. However, some towns had much more active printing and publishing trades than others. At least half of the two thousand editions were printed in just five towns—Venice, Italy; Rome, Italy; Leipzig, Germany; Paris, France; and Lyons, France.

INCUNABULA:
THE INFANCY OF PRINTING

According to lists compiled by modern librarians, nearly thirty thousand works were printed in movable type before the end of the 1500s. These early printed books, pamphlets, and broadsides are referred to as incunabula, the Latin term for the bands used to hold a baby in the cradle and a metaphor for the earliest stages of any new development.

How many individual items were printed during the incunabular period? No one can say precisely because we do not know the number of copies made of each title. Estimates vary widely. Some print runs were small, two hundred or three hundred copies. But an ambitious publisher who printed a popular *World Chronicle* in Nuremberg, Germany, in 1493 turned out more than two thousand copies, some in Latin and some in German. The total number of incunabula, one recent

SCRIPT AND PRINT COEXIST

Opposition to the new art of printing flared up in Genoa, Italy; Augsburg, Germany; and Paris, France. Some scribes wanted their jobs protected by laws prohibiting printers from issuing prayer books and school texts. Snobbish book collectors looked down their noses at printed books and purchased only handwritten works for their libraries. So large numbers of handwritten books continued to be produced.

Printed and handwritten books were sold in the same bookshops and fairs, and occasionally, printed and handwritten quires were bound together in one volume. They were the same product in

Gutenberg biographer suggests, could be 9 million. Some other scholars estimate it at 15 or 20 million books.

These numbers do not sound large today, when a single publisher might print 12 million copies of an expected best-seller (the first print run of the U.S. edition of *Harry Potter and the Deathly Hallows* in 2007). But compared to the publication rate of late medieval scriptoria, the number of books printed in the late fifteenth century is astounding. In the time it took six scribes to produce six copies of a book, six printers could produce hundreds of copies.

The printed copies had the advantage not just of numbers but of being identical. People marveled at the accuracy most people's eyes. The printed book was not something new and different. It was simply a cheaper, more swiftly produced, and probably more accurate copy.

By 1475 manuscript production was declining. But printing did not put scribes out of work. Some, such as Schöffer, became printers. Others became rubricators or used their skills at calligraphy to provide designs for punch cutters to make new type. Most continued writing by hand documents that did not need multiple copies: court records, government archives, commercial ledgers, and business letters. The scribe did not disappear in Europe until the late nineteenth century when the typewriter took over. Calligraphers remain in demand for elegant invitations, diplomas, and unique editions of books.

of books produced by the printing press: "When the impression is correct," an Italian scholar commented in 1475, "it runs through all the copies in the same order, with scarcely the possibility of error—a thing which in a manuscript is apt to result quite differently."

Equally impressive was the price. A bishop writing a preface to a book published in Rome in 1468 pointed out that "volumes which in former times could scarce be bought for a hundred gold pieces are today to be had for reading in good versions and free of faults throughout for twenty." He added that "one can hardly report inventions of like importance for mankind, whether in ancient or modern times."

A TIMELY INVENTION

Gutenberg could not have developed his invention at a better time. Europe was primed for the printing press. Its success was propelled by a variety of factors. Paper was being widely manufactured, providing an inexpensive substitute for the animal skins that had supplied the chief writing materials for centuries. Capitalism—an economic system based on the monetary wealth of private individuals or groups of individuals—was beginning to replace feudalism, the land-based wealth of nobility and royalty. As commerce expanded, new banking practices eased the way for loans and investments in the new printing industry.

The Roman Catholic Church, whose influence spanned Europe, avidly supported printing. A variety of religious manuals were needed for church services and for the education of priests, and the church wanted them to be uniform and correct. Printing greatly helped fund-raising through the sale of letters of indulgence. The church also oversaw the universities, where students needed textbooks and where scholars, eagerly rediscovering the works of ancient writers, prepared editions of Roman and Greek classics.

Literacy, moreover, was no longer limited to the clergy. More and more Europeans not training for or employed by the church were learning to read and write. Merchants, women, knights, and nobles were reading books for information and entertainment. And eyeglasses—first developed in Europe in the thirteenth century—made it possible for all kinds of readers to enjoy books into old age. Before Gutenberg's invention, both monasteries and commercial scriptoria were producing large numbers of

As reading became more popular in Europe, so did eyeglasses. The eyeglass frames shown above were made in the late fifteenth century.

manuscript books, but scribes could not keep up with the demand.

With the arrival of printing, books flooded the market. The majority—nearly 80 percent—were Latin works, almost half of them religious in nature. Bibles, many based on Gutenberg's 42-line version, poured off the presses. Classical works by such writers as Aristotle, Julius Caesar, Cicero, Euclid, Horace, Livy, Ovid, and Virgil also appeared frequently. As early as 1466, printers began printing the Bible in German to reach a wider audience. People could also buy popular chronicles and chivalric romances (adventure stories about knights) in German, Italian, French, Flemish, or English. Students could at last afford textbooks. Among the many books available were "how to read" manuals to help everyone cope with the information overload.

THE IMPACT OF PRINT

The impact of the new technology on European society was swift and powerful. The greater production capacity of print totally changed the book trade. The small, local retail business in commissioned manuscripts became an international market of printed books, often produced on speculation— without an order from a specific buyer. Booksellers carried their wares from town to town by boat or horseback. Printed books became a regular feature at annual trade fairs, such as the one in Frankfurt, where Aeneas Piccolomini, the papal legate, first viewed pages from Gutenberg's Bible.

The effect on education was also striking. Even though schools still depended on lectures and rote learning as the main teaching tools, pupils for the first time had the opportunity to learn on their own by reading books. As a

This sixteenth-century illustration shows a crowded and busy classroom. The children in the center of the picture all hold their own copies of a schoolbook as they read aloud to the teacher.

Venetian historian commented in 1483, "Why should old men be preferred to their juniors now that it is possible for the young by diligent study to acquire the same knowledge?" Smart students, such as the Danish astronomer Tycho Brahe (1546–1601), could sneak books past their tutors to expand their knowledge of the world. People had more choice to pursue subjects that interested them, not just what a teacher wanted them to study.

Print especially benefited the spread of scientific knowledge. Before Gutenberg, scientists often made their own copies of their work to avoid the errors scribes made when copying unfamiliar material. After printing was invented, scientists could oversee the printing process, proofreading and correcting galleys before copies were printed. The printed book was more accurate, and these accurate copies could be sent to colleagues working at other centers of learning. Scientists in different cities could then confer by mail knowing that each had an identical copy of a treatise. Time saved by not having to make individual copies of their work gave scientists more time for new research.

The addition of woodcut (and later copperplate) illustrations to text set in movable type (a process Albrecht Pfister pioneered in 1461) opened the possibility of inserting botanical and anatomical sketches, technical diagrams, and maps into scientific books. Technical data could also be typeset in tables for quick consultation. For the first time, images, maps, and diagrams in a book were the same in every copy.

Printers helped readers find information quickly by using indexes, page numbers, and running headers (the chapter title and book title repeated alternately at the top or side of each page), features already familiar from manuscript books. They introduced the practice of printing title pages. These helped identify works by one uniform title instead of the many different titles often given to the same work by scribes copying manuscripts.

Errors, of course, crept into printed books. The Dutch philosopher Erasmus (1466–1536) complained about the mistakes of careless printers. "In earlier times," he noted, "a single writing mistake would only affect one copy, but now it appears in an edition of thousands." But one advantage of printing was that when an error occurred, the chances of finding it were increased because so many more people were reading each edition of a work.

The broad advances in scientific knowledge during the sixteenth, seventeenth, and eighteenth centuries as well as the telescope, the microscope, and other inventions that made such discoveries possible were all aided by the print revolution.

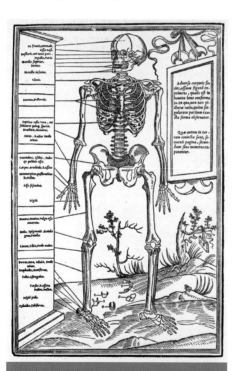

A page from a sixteenth-century anatomy book features a diagram of a human skeleton. The availability of printed books aided many scientific advances.

THE PROTESTANT REFORMATION

The political impact of print was immediately obvious. As early as 1461, the two rival archbishops of Mainz saw the advantages of printing fliers to sway public opinion. Since the invention of printing was a private endeavor, not financed by the church or a secular ruler, the press was free at the start. Fust and Schöffer, keeping their personal loyalties in the conflict to themselves, printed propaganda for both factions. When Adolf II of Nassau won the struggle and sent Gutenberg and many other Mainz residents into exile, he allowed Fust and Schöffer to continue in business in Mainz. Evidently Adolf recognized their usefulness. Later,

This sixteenth-century illustration shows a scene from Peter Schöffer's Mainz print shop. Schöffer printed propaganda for both sides in the archbishops' war of 1462.

his praise for and rewards to Gutenberg also reflected his awareness of the political value of the press.

Protests against corruption in the Roman Catholic Church were not new. Up until the invention of printing, however, the church generally succeeded in suppressing dissident voices by resorting to trials for heresy, executions, and crusades against its critics. John Wyclif was a fourteenth-century English theologian who supported many reforms, including translating the Bible into English so that more people could read it. For that, he was condemned as a

NEWSPAPERS

On November 7, 1492, shortly before noon, a 260-pound (118-kilogram) meteorite fell into Earth's atmosphere. It crashed into a wheat field near the German town of Ensishem with a big bang heard 75 miles (121 km) away. The event inspired Sebastian Brant, a law professor at the University of Basel and a talented writer, to publish a one-page, illustrated account. In Latin and German verses, he put a political twist on the incident, claiming it was a divine sign that the Holy Roman emperor should attack the king of France.

Brant's broadside is the earliest survivor of many similar sheets reporting sensational news. Deformed pigs, disasters, and battles were among the subjects of these fliers. Others carried royal proclamations of the sort that heralds had formerly made

heretic and his followers were persecuted. The Czech theologian Jan Hus, who was inspired by Wyclif's ideas, was
burned at the stake in 1415.

But in the early sixteenth century, Martin Luther, the
German leader of the Protestant Reformation, used the press
to overcome the suppressive tactics of the church. He took a
very public stand against the sale of indulgences and other
church practices that he felt corrupted the true spirit of
Christianity. Luther, too, might have been silenced had the
printing press not made his writings widely available. From

public by reading handwritten scrolls in public squares. These
publications were small and limited in scope. Like the calendars
Gutenberg printed in the 1450s and 1460s, these early news
sheets included astrology, popular medicine, and other advice.
And as with Gutenberg's Turkish calendar and Brant's account of
the meteorite, they sometimes espoused political opinions and
predictions.

Regularly published newspapers developed in the seventeenth
century, first in the Netherlands and later in other European
countries. Many encountered censorship from church or state
authorities, but neither the church nor the state could totally
suppress the popular medium. Gradually, in the eighteenth
century, European newspapers began to win the legal right to
freely publish news and opinions.

Martin Luther (shown in a painting from 1882) saw the value of the printing press in spreading his message of religious reform. He published a Bible in German, as well as many tracts, sermons, pamphlets, hymns, and fliers.

the "ninety-five theses" of 1517—his first list of protests—Luther published a steady stream of tracts, sermons, pamphlets, hymns, and fliers explaining and defending his views. By 1520 his most important tracts were available in Dutch, English, Spanish, Czech, and Latin. In 1521 his masterful translation of the New Testament into a readable and widely accessible German was an immediate success. By 1534 he had completed the Old Testament as well. He wrote so prolifically and printers issued his work so steadily that in the first half of the sixteenth century, one-third of all books printed in German were written by Martin Luther.

Efforts by the church to suppress Luther's writings were fruitless. Too many presses, too many booksellers, and too many trade routes made it impossible for the church to prevent the dissemination of printed matter it opposed.

Before Luther's death in 1546, about half of Germany's territories had broken away from Roman Catholic control.

Luther's success inspired other reformers to organize other Protestant churches. These included the reformed churches of Huldreich Zwingli and John Calvin in Switzerland, John Knox in Scotland, and state religions independent of Rome in Sweden, Denmark, Norway, the Netherlands, and England. A more radical religious reformation by a movement called the Anabaptists also rebelled against state control of religion. Although economic and other factors contributed to these major social changes, a key role was played by the rapid spread of views critical of the Roman Catholic Church made possible by printing presses.

A GLOBAL PHENOMENON

The ripples of Gutenberg's invention spread. Printing was no longer a German phenomenon or even a European one. In the late fifteenth century and through the sixteenth, printing spread to Istanbul, Turkey; Fez, Morocco; Goa, India; and Nagasaki, Japan. The Spaniards took printing across the Atlantic to Mexico and Lima, Peru.

Not only was the press spreading outward from Europe, printing was making Europeans more knowledgeable about the rest of the world. Travel accounts, which had long been popular, became more quickly and widely available. The letters of Christopher Columbus and Hernán Cortés about the New World appeared in print as early as 1493 and 1522, respectively. New maps, charts, geographies, and natural histories were printed and disseminated, inspiring explorers and travelers to venture into distant places to trade and to conquer.

The overseas empires of Spain, Portugal, France, England, the Netherlands, and other European nations both depended on printed information and produced it. Accounts of the riches of Asia and America helped dissatisfied and adventurous Europeans decide to pull up roots and resettle in faraway lands.

Printed books brought world cultures closer together. Through print, people in conquered lands learned European languages and literature, religious practices, science, and mathematics. Printed books also recorded the Asian, African, and Native American languages and customs of conquered people for Europeans to study.

REVOLUTIONS

The print revolution also aided political revolutions in the late eighteenth and early nineteenth centuries. Earlier European philosophers such as John Locke (1632–1704) and Jean-Jacques Rousseau (1712–1778) questioned the absolute power of monarchs. People had the right, they argued, to choose how they were governed. Educated people read about these new ideas in books. Tracts, handbills, and newspapers carried them to an even wider public.

The British colonies of North America had only a small population of European descent in the eighteenth century. It was scattered over a large area. Newspapers brought the colonists information and fostered a sense of community. The papers were also an important source of income for printers, who also organized a postal system for their delivery. By the time the American Revolution (1775–1783) began, every one of the thirteen colonies that rebelled against British rule had presses (among them Benjamin Franklin's press in Philadelphia). Newspapers and pamphlets such as Thomas Paine's *Common Sense* played an important role in gathering support for the Revolution and winning the colonies' independence from Great Britain.

The printing press similarly helped free Latin America and France from rule by royalty. As the revolutionary orator Anacharsis Cloots declared in a speech to the National Assembly during the French Revolution (1789–1799), "Gutenberg's invention will become the tool with which we will rework the future." And as German scientist Christoph Lichtenberg observed during that same era, "The lead in typecases has changed the world more than the lead in bullets."

COMMON SENSE:

ADDRESSED TO THE

INHABITANTS

OF

A M E R I C A.

On the following interesting

S U B J E C T S.

I. Of the Origin and Design of Government in general, with concise Remarks on the English Constitution.

II. Of Monarchy and Hereditary Succession.

III. Thoughts on the present State of American Affairs.

IV. Of the present Ability of America, with some miscellaneous Reflections.

Written by an ENGLISHMAN.

By Thomas Paine

Man knows no Master save creating HEAVEN,
Or those whom choice and common good ordain.
THOMSON.

PHILADELPHIA, Printed
And Sold by R. BELL, in Third-Street, 1776.

Common Sense, *Thomas Paine's pamphlet outlining his persuasive argument for independence from Great Britain, sold more than 100,000 copies in the first few months of publication.*

THE IMPACT OF PRINT

Martin Luther called printing "God's highest and most extreme gift, by which the business of the Gospel is driven forward." In the nineteenth century, French novelist Victor Hugo said, "The invention of printing is the greatest event in history. It is the mother of revolution. It is the mode of expression of humanity which is totally renewed; it is human thought stripping off one form and donning another. . . ." Nineteenth-century American writer Mark Twain said, "What the world is today, good and bad, it owes to Gutenberg. Everything can be traced to this source, but we are bound to bring him homage, . . . for the bad that his colossal invention has brought about is overshadowed a thousand times by the good with which mankind has been favored."

Into the nineteenth and twentieth centuries, the printing press continued to have a great impact on the development of the nations of modern Europe and their colonies around the world. Print was not the direct cause of all the scientific, technological, religious, and political changes of these centuries, but it made the world a smaller place and sped them along.

LATER DEVELOPMENTS

The age of Gutenberg—the era of printed books—has lasted more than five hundred years. The old methods of typecasting and printing that Gutenberg first created finally began to change in the nineteenth century as new inventions improved their efficiency. Steam-powered presses, invented in 1811, freed printers from the job of pulling hard on the lever for each printed page. By mid-century, inventors had devised ways to put the printing plate on a cylinder. Later improvements added a second cylinder, so that a continuous roll of paper could run between the cylinders, printing both sides of a sheet at once. In 1884 a mechanical typesetting machine called the Linotype made obsolete the slow placement of individual pieces of type on a compositor's stick. Instead of lining up each letter by hand, the compositor could type the text at a keyboard and let the machine put the pieces of type in place.

In the mid-twentieth century, two different inventions eliminated the need for metal type. Photography, first developed in the nineteenth century, provided a way to use film to reproduce printed pages. Instead of using metal type, a machine called a phototypesetter projected light through a film negative image of an individual character in a font onto film. A lens magnified or reduced the character to the size desired. Another invention developed at about the same time was xerography (also known as photocopying). This process simplified the reproduction of printed texts by using electrostatic energy.

Meanwhile, inventors were developing computers and laser printers in the 1980s. By the 1990s, businesses, schools, and homes were using these machines for a variety of small printing jobs. Desktop publishing was also replacing the bulky machines formerly needed for preparing an original copy for printing fliers, pamphlets, newspapers, magazines, and books.

Modern printers can make a printing plate directly

THE SPEED OF CHANGE

Modern innovations in technology expand far more quickly than they did in Gutenberg's day. A U.S. government report, "The Emerging Digital Economy," remarks on how quickly people embraced the Internet. "The Internet's pace of adoption," the report reads, "eclipses all other technologies that preceded it. Radio was in existence 38 years before 50 million people tuned in; TV took 13 years to reach that benchmark. Sixteen years after the first PC kit came out, 50 million people were using one. Once it was opened to the general public, the Internet crossed that line in four years."

from a computer file. They then use a process called offset printing. First, the images and text are put on a printing plate, usually made of aluminum. The plate is inked and the information transferred to a rubber blanket. Copies are then printed from the blanket.

Computer networks and the Internet have made it possible to bypass printing words on paper altogether. These inventions are transforming our world as much as the printing press changed Gutenberg's. Whole libraries are being digitized to make centuries of information available to millions of readers at the click of a mouse. E-books and e-zines are published online. A multivolume encyclopedia or dictionary can fit on one compact disc. For much of our reading, the computer screen is replacing the printed page.

Yet we still live in an age of print. Printed signs, advertisements, and labels supply us with information everywhere we look. Interest in font design remains strong, especially since anyone can design a new typeface with software, rather than by spending a day carving each punch. Even on the computer screen we are constantly reading print.

Books will probably never cease to be printed, just as handwritten notes and letters did not disappear when printing became possible. But only the future will tell the direction our new inventions will take us and how the current communications revolution will affect us, our science, our political structures, and our lives.

One of the earliest tributes to Johannes Gutenberg was written December 31, 1470, by the rector of the University of Paris. "Not far from the city of Mainz, there appeared a certain Johannes whose surname was Gutenberg, who, first of all men, devised the art of printing, whereby books are made, not by a reed, as did the ancients, nor with a quill pen, as do we, but with metal letters, and that swiftly, neatly, beautifully," he wrote. "Surely this man is worthy to be loaded with divine honors by all the Muses, all the arts, all the tongues of those who delight in books, and is all the more to be preferred to gods and goddesses in that he has put the means of choice within the reach of letters themselves and of mortals devoted to culture. That great Gutenberg has discovered things far more pleasing and divine, in carving out letters in such a fashion that whatever can be said or thought can by them be written down at once and transcribed and committed to the memory of posterity." Book lovers can only agree with honoring the man who patiently, through years of trial and error, worked out the process that made books available for the whole world.

PRIMARY SOURCE RESEARCH

To learn about historical events, people study many sources, such as books, newspaper articles, websites, photographs, and paintings. These sources can be separated into two general categories—primary sources and secondary sources.

A primary source is the record of an eyewitness. Primary sources provide firsthand accounts about a person or event. Examples include diaries, letters, autobiographies, speeches, newspapers, and oral history interviews. Libraries, archives, historical societies, and museums often have primary sources available on-site or on the Internet.

A secondary source is published information that was researched, collected, and written or otherwise created by someone who was not an eyewitness. These authors or artists use primary sources and other secondary sources in their research, but they interpret and arrange the source material in their own works. Secondary sources include history books, novels, biographies, movies, documentaries, and magazines. Libraries and museums are filled with secondary sources.

After finding primary and secondary sources, authors and historians must evaluate them. They may ask questions such as: Who created this document? What is this person's point of view? What biases might this person have? How trustworthy is this document? Just because a person was an eyewitness to an event does not mean that person recorded the whole truth about that event. For example, a soldier describing a battle might depict only the heroic actions of his unit and only the brutal behavior of the enemy. An account from a soldier on the opposing side might portray the same battle very differently. When sources disagree, researchers must decide through additional study which explanation makes the most sense. For this reason, historians consult a variety of primary and secondary sources. Then they can draw their own conclusions.

The Pivotal Moments in History series takes readers on a journey to important junctures in history that shaped our modern world. Authors researched each event using both primary and secondary sources, an approach that enhances readers' awareness of the complexities of the materials and helps bring to life rich stories from which we draw our understanding of our shared history.

LEARNING ABOUT GUTENBERG

Almost everything we know about Johannes Gutenberg and how he invented the printing press in fifteenth-century Europe comes from three types of primary material. First are the works that Gutenberg (and other early printers) printed. Second are the documents from Gutenberg's time that mention Gutenberg by name. Third are references to Gutenberg and the invention of printing in books written soon after his death by people who knew him or knew of him from his colleagues. Like detectives solving a mystery, scholars have pieced together these sources into an account that persuasively establishes the main outlines of Gutenberg's life and achievement. It has not been an easy task.

THE PRODUCTS OF GUTENBERG'S PRESS

The best evidence of Gutenberg's achievement is his work, the books, pamphlets, and other printed papers that came off his press. The most splendid is the masterpiece of printing known as the Gutenberg Bible. Fragments of earlier works and single-page printing jobs reveal the development of the new craft. Later works show him mastering new, smaller typefaces for more efficient communication of knowledge.

We can all admire these documents through printed photographs, in museums, and on the Internet. But many of us cannot read the inside story they reveal of Gutenberg's work, for understanding these primary sources requires professional printing expertise and scientific analysis of metals, paper, and inks. We must depend on secondary sources, books written by art historians, printers, scientists, and other scholars who can interpret these primary sources for us.

FINDING THE MAN

Imagine combing through town records in the cities where Gutenberg is known to have lived looking for mentions of Johannes Gutenberg. He might appear under that name, but he might also be referred to as Henchen zu Gutenberg (Johnny of Gutenberg) or Hengin, Henne, Henchin, Hannsse, or Johan. His last name may appear with or without the *zu*, may be spelled Gudenberg or Guttenberg or Gutemberg, or may be some version of Gensfleisch, the surname his father used. We can be certain all of these names apply because some references helpfully fill out the picture by adding on other indicators, as in "Johann Gensefleisch the younger, called Gutemberg."

In fifteenth-century Germany, people were generally known by their first names. To distinguish themselves from other people with the same first name (and Johannes, like John in English, was a very popular name), they added the house they lived in. When people traveled to another place, they might identify themselves by the town they came from. Town records in Strasbourg, for example refer to Gutenberg as Hans (or Johan) Gutenberg "of Mainz."

How names were spelled generally reflected the dialect and spelling habits of the scribe writing the document. Since none of the surviving documents bears Gutenberg's signature and he did not print his name in any of the books issued by his press, we have no idea how he himself spelled his name.

THE GUTENBERG DOCUMENTS

Gutenberg left little evidence of his life and work behind. The lack of notebooks sketching Gutenberg's plans may be due to the secrecy of his project. In a time with no patent laws to protect inventions, Gutenberg must have been careful to leave no record of his experiments.

But over several centuries, scholars have teased some one hundred references to Gutenberg out of about two dozen legal records, account books, political charters, tax assessments, sales contracts, and membership lists of organizations. Curiously, all of these early documents mentioning the inventor of printing were not printed but handwritten. Hence they are not found in multiple copies.

Many of the original documents recording details about Gutenberg's life and work were destroyed or lost. War and other disasters probably played a role in many of these losses. Armies looted both Strasbourg and Mainz in Gutenberg's lifetime, and the Thirty Years War (1618–1648) brought widespread devastation to Gutenberg's homeland.

Luckily for those curious about Gutenberg, a few eighteenth-century scholars ferreted out references to him and made copies or notes of what they read. The first collection of printed documents concerning Gutenberg was published in 1760. It is fortunate that efforts to record information about Gutenberg began before the French Revolution. When French forces occupied Strasbourg in 1793, they celebrated with bonfires fueled by pages from the town archives.

Later, during the Franco-Prussian War (1870–1871), Germany fought to regain possession of the Rhineland. More documents were lost when the Strasbourg city library went up in flames during a battle. Other documents have simply disappeared, possibly stolen or merely misplaced. In 1925 a German scholar, Karl Schorbach, collected and published all the known references to Gutenberg made during his lifetime. In 1941 Douglas McMurtrie translated them all from German and Latin into English.

These Gutenberg documents are like pieces in a very incomplete jigsaw puzzle. They give us glimpses of his social and professional status, his financial dealings, four lawsuits (two of which we do not know the outcome of), and some of his tax payments. The small details of daily life that emerge are fascinating, but the big question— exactly when and how did he perfect the process of printing with movable type?—is left for us to figure out from the works he printed.

THE INVENTOR OF PRINTING WITH MOVABLE TYPES

Gutenberg did not put his name on any of the printed works we attribute to him. So how do we know he invented the printing press?

The third group of documents offers assurance that Johannes Gutenberg was indeed the wizard who put together a variety of technical skills to create the method of reproducing writing that took Europe by storm in the mid-fifteenth century. A variety of documents by a cousin, a former partner, other early printers, chronicle writers who interviewed printers, and even a decree by King Charles VII of France, all vouch for Gutenberg as the inventor.

LOOKING FOR ARTIFACTS

A fourth source of information about Gutenberg would be portraits, equipment he used, and any other objects that would reveal something about him and his work. Unfortunately, nothing of this kind survives.

All the paintings and statues of Gutenberg that still exist were created long after he died, the earliest nearly one hundred years later. They may not look anything like him. Most images show him with a full, long beard, a style that was shunned by Germans of Gutenberg's patrician class during the mid-fifteenth century. Gentlemen, merchants, and tradesmen of Gutenberg's day were clean shaven or wore neatly clipped short beards. Did the later artists show him with a beard to make him look more distinguished?

Nothing remains of the mold he invented to make type, the presses he developed to apply pressure evenly to the sheets atop the inked type, or the type itself. By looking at woodcuts picturing printers at work, however, we can imagine what the tools Gutenberg used might have looked like.

The earliest surviving illustration of a print shop was published in Lyon, France, in 1499. The book is a religious work, and the purpose of the picture is not to explain the printing process but to warn readers to be prepared for death. Even though macabre skeletons dominate the picture, we do get an idea of how printers worked nearly fifty years after Gutenberg's invention.

We can learn more about how printing was done from a surviving sixteenth-century press and old typecasting molds. Curators at the Gutenberg Museum in Mainz have built a press and molds like the old ones to show visitors the processes Gutenberg likely used to create type and print pages. Since few changes were made in printing technology during the first four hundred years, even later printing presses can help us understand the work involved. Many print shops and printing museums in the United States offer visitors a hands-on experience. You can set the type, apply the ink, align the paper, and slide it all under the flat plate of the press. Then you pull the lever old-time printers call the devil's tail for the thrill of a Gutenberg moment in a post-Gutenberg age.

A PASSAGE FROM GUTENBERG'S BIBLE

Dominus regit me et nichil michi deerit : in loco pascue ibi me collocauit. Super aquam refectionis educauit me : animam meam conuertit. Deduxit me super semitas iustitie : propter nomen suum. Nam et si ambulauero in medio umbre mortis non timebo mala : quoniam tu mecum es. Virga tua et baculus tuus : ipsa me consolata sunt. Parasti in conspectu meo mensam : aduersus eos qui tribulant me. Impinguasti in oleo caput meum : et calix meus inebrians quam preclarus est. Et misericordia tua subsequetur me : omnibus diebus uite mee. Et ut inhabitem in domo domini : in longitudine dierum.

This printing of Psalm 23 (above) comes from a Bible printed by Gutenberg in Mainz, Germany, in 1454 or 1455.

IN LATIN:

Dominus regit me et nihil mihi deerit : in loco pascuae ibi me collocavit. Super aquam refectionis educavit me : animam meam convertit. Deduxit me super semitas justiciae : propter nomen suum. Nam et si ambulavero in medio umbrae mortis non timebo mala : quoniam tu mecum es. Virga tua et baculus tuus : ipsa me consolata sunt. Parasti in conspectu meo mensam : adversus eos qui tribulant me. Impinguasti in oleo caput meum : et calix meus inebrians quam praeclarus est. Et misericordia tua subsequetur me omnibus diebus vitae meae : et ut inhabitem in domo domini: in longitudinem dierum.

IN ENGLISH:

The Lord rules me, and to me nothing is lacking. He has set me in a place of pasture. On the water of refreshment, he has raised me. He has converted my soul. He leads me on the paths of justice, for his name's sake. Even if I should walk in the shadow of death, I shall not fear evils because you are with me. Your rod and your staff—these have comforted me. You have prepared my table in the sight of those who afflict me. You have anointed my head with oil, and my chalice inebriates me—how splendid it is! And your mercy shall follow me all the days of my life, and so that I may inhabit the house of the Lord the length of days [for eternity].

The Book of Psalms appears at the end of volume I of Gutenberg's Bible. Each psalm opens with an initial letter two lines tall. Gutenberg left the space blank when he printed the pages, and a rubricator wrote these initials by hand in red ink. It was not yet the custom to number verses in Bibles. But each verse of the psalm is indicated with another, smaller handwritten capital. In some copies, the rubricator alternated between red and blue ink.

Historians do not know what manuscript Gutenberg used as a model. Scholars have suggested that it was a small format manuscript because some of the mistakes in printing occurred when a compositor misunderstood an abbreviation. All handwritten books used abbreviations. People expected them in books, and so Gutenberg used many of them in printing the Bible. Since it was not then the custom to indicate abbreviations with a period, as we do, Gutenberg had to make special types for the symbols scribes used when shortening words.

A short wavy line above a letter usually means that the next letter (or two or three) is missing. In the third line, for example, the mark over the final letter in *aqua* is an abbreviation for the letter *m*. You can find many similar marks in almost every verse of the psalm. Several stand for *m* or *n*, but others replace *s*, *er*, and *rae*. Another abbreviation looks like a small number 9, placed at the end of a word ending in *us*. The opening word *Dominus* (God) is abbreviated Domin9. (The rubricator used the same symbol for the *us* in "psalmus.") In the fifth line, a double *p* (which is a ligature—a type with two characters) is an abbreviation for the "prop" in propter. A special symbol, perhaps an ancestor of the plus sign, stands for *et* (and) in line 9.

Gutenberg also followed scribal practice in his punctuation. The psalm has colons separating the clauses within sentences and periods at the end of sentences. This simple marking shows the balanced phrasing of the Hebrew original. The dots on the *i*'s imitate the handwritten custom of using little crescents. The great variety of these marks has led to the proposal that Gutenberg did not use metal matrices when casting type but a separate mold made of sand or clay for each individual type.

TIMELINE

CA. 1390   First paper mill in Germany is established near Nuremberg.

CA. 1400   Johannes Gutenberg is born.

1403   King Taejong of Korea sets up a printing house with hundreds of thousands of pieces of type made from bronze.

1418–1420   "Johannes de Altavilla" studies at Erfurt University.

1428   Guild members take over leadership of Mainz City Council. Gutenberg is probably among the many patricians who leave Mainz in protest.

1434   In Strasbourg, Gutenberg has Mainz city clerk Niklaus Wörstadt arrested for not paying him annuities owed him by Mainz.

1436   Hanns Dünne, a goldsmith, receives one hundred gulden from Gutenberg "solely for that which pertains to the use of a press."

1437   Two plaintiffs sue Gutenberg, one for breach of promise of marriage and the other for libel.

1438   Gutenberg forms a partnership with Andreas Dritzehn, Andreas Heilman, and Hans Riffe.

1439	Andreas Dritzehn's brothers sue Gutenberg for Andreas's share of the partnership. On December 12, the judge rules that Gutenberg owes Andreas's brothers only fifteen gulden.
1444	Gutenberg pays his wine tax on March 12. This is the last surviving evidence of his residence in Strasbourg.
1448	Gutenberg begins printing Donatuses and other small jobs.
CA. 1450	Gutenberg establishes a partnership with Johann Fust. Together they set up a shop for the "work of the books."
CA. 1452–1455	Gutenberg prints the 42-line Bible.
1454	In October Aeneas Sylvius Piccolomini (a papal legate and later Pope Pius II) sees quires of Gutenberg's Bible being offered for sale at the Frankfurt fair.
1454–1455	Gutenberg prints indulgences to raise money to defend Cyprus from the Turks and a calendar that is also a political tract.
1455	On November 6, a notary witnesses Fust's oath that he borrowed money, at interest, to lend to Gutenberg. This ends Fust's suit against Gutenberg. Fust wins control over all

of the printing equipment purchased and manufactured for "the work of the books."

1456	In August Heinrich Cremer, a Mainz clergyman, writes a note that he has completed the rubrication, illumination, and binding of a two-volume copy of the Bible printed by Gutenberg.
	Gutenberg prints a papal bull calling for a crusade against the Turks and a calendar containing medical advice.
1457	On August 14, Fust and Peter Schöffer issue the Mainz Psalter, which includes the first printed colophon. Gutenberg continues printing various small jobs.
1458	Gutenberg fails to pay interest on a loan from St. Thomas Church in Strasbourg.
1458–61	Printing spreads beyond Mainz to Bamberg and Strasbourg. Gutenberg prints the *Catholicon*. Fust and Schöffer issue more psalters, missals, and other books.
1462	After the archbishops' war in Mainz, Gutenberg is exiled, perhaps to Eltville.

1465	On Janunary 14, Gutenberg is appointed courtier by Adolf II of Nassau, archbishop of Mainz. Two Germans, Konrad Sweynheym and Arnold Pannartz, begin printing works in Subiaco, near Rome.
1465–1467	The Bechtermünze brothers print *Vocabularius ex quo* in Eltville.
1466	Ulrich Zell begins printing in Cologne.
1467	Printing begins in Rome.
1468	Gutenberg dies on February 3. Three weeks later, Dr. Konrad Humery acknowledges receipt of printing equipment from the Gutenberg estate. Printing spreads to Augsburg.
1469	Printing reaches Venice.
1470	Print shops open in Naples, Italy; Nuremberg, Germany; and Paris, France.
1472	Printing spreads to Basel.
1473	William Caxton prints the first printed book in English, *The Recuyell of the Historyes of Troye*, in Bruges, Belgium.
1476	Caxton sets up the first English press at Westminster. In 1478 he publishes the first printed version of Chaucer's *Canterbury Tales*.

GLOSSARY

BLOCK PRINTING: the printing of images or text using a block of wood or a metal plate with a picture or writing carved in relief and in reverse

BROADSIDE: a large sheet of paper or vellum printed only on one side

CHARACTER: a graphic symbol, such as a letter of the alphabet, a hieroglyph, or an ideogram, used in printing

COLOPHON: a note written or printed at the end of a work by the scribe or printer who made the copy. It typically includes information about when and where the work was produced.

COMPOSITOR: the worker who selects individual pieces of type from a case and sets them up on a compositor's stick in the correct order for each line to be printed. This person is also called a typesetter.

DIE: a tool, similar to a punch, made of a hard material (such as steel) with a design, picture, or writing carved in reverse into it. Dies are used to copy that design, picture, or writing onto a softer material by pressure or by a blow.

FONT: a set of type or characters all of one style and size

FORM: the printing type arranged and secured in a frame and ready for printing

FRISKET: a protective frame placed around an area to be printed to keep the margins of the page from being smudged

MANUSCRIPT: a handwritten book

MATRIX: a mold from which a relief surface (such as a piece of type) is made. The plural is *matrices*.

PARCHMENT: writing material prepared from an animal skin

PLATEN: the flat metal plate of a printing press that presses the paper or vellum against the inked type

PUNCH: a tool made of a hard material (such as steel) with a design, picture, or writing carved in relief and in reverse on one end. By placing the punch against a softer material such as copper and striking it with a hammer, printers produced matrices, the molds used to make individual pieces of type.

QUIRE: four or five sheets of paper or vellum folded in half and placed one inside the other to create a booklet of sixteen or twenty pages

SCRIPTORIUM: a room in a monastery or a commercial shop where scribes copied books. The plural is *scriptoria*.

TYMPAN: on a printing press, the flat wooden tray that holds the paper or vellum. It is hinged to fold over the inked type.

VELLUM: the skin of a young animal that is scraped and prepared for writing or printing, finer than parchment. The word is from *vitellus* (Latin for "small calf"). Modern vellum, also called parchment, is a thick, translucent, cream-colored paper.

WHO'S WHO?

NICHOLAS JENSON (1420–1480) Born in Sommevoire, France, Jenson was the "man dextrous in engraving" whom Charles VII of France sent to Mainz in 1458 to learn the art of printing. Jenson succeeded in his mission. But Charles died in 1461, while Jenson was in Germany. Charles's son and successor, Louis XI, dismissed all the court officials his father had appointed. When the new king refused to compensate Jenson for his work or to provide money for Jenson to establish a printing office in Paris, Jenson did not return to France. Some scholars suggest that he spent a few years at a monastery of the Brethren of the Common Life in Marienthal, near Mainz, cutting punches to make type. In 1468 the monks began printing indulgences. Later, Jenson went to Venice, where he opened his own workshop in 1470 and became famous for designing a new roman typeface from which all later roman types are derived.

JOHANN MENTELIN (CA. 1410–1478) By the 1440s, Strasbourg-born Mentelin was working in the city as a manuscript illuminator—an artist who decorated handwritten books with gold and silver leaf and brilliant colors. It is possible he met Gutenberg in Strasbourg and went with him to Mainz to train as a printer. About 1458 he was setting up his own print shop in Strasbourg. The Mentelin Bible in 1460 was the second printed edition of the Bible and the first book printed in Strasbourg. He went on to publish about forty books, including Latin works of theology and philosophy (by such authors as Saint Augustine and Saint Thomas Aquinas), classical works (by Virgil, Terence, and Aristotle), and German courtly literature (such as Wolfram von Eschenbach's *Parzival*). In 1466 he printed the first German translation of the Bible, which before Luther's translation (1534) became the model for about thirteen later editions by various printers in south Germany.

NICHOLAS OF CUSA (1401–1464) Nicholas was a brilliant German philosopher, scientist, and mathematician. He was also a major leader of the Roman Catholic Church. As a papal legate and later as a bishop and a cardinal, he worked tirelessly for church unity and reform. Nicholas's many writings include treatises on law, theology, astronomy, mathematics, and philosophy. Well before Copernicus (1473–1543), he held that the earth is not the center of the universe but revolves around the sun. He was also an early advocate of the calendar reform that was not enacted until Pope Gregory XIII did so in 1582.

In a preface to a book printed in Rome in 1468, Giovanni Andrea Bussi, Nicholas's former secretary, noted that Nicholas took a personal interest in Gutenberg and his invention. Nicholas, he wrote, "had the fervent desire to see this holy art [of printing], which began in Germany, also established in Rome."

AENEAS SYLVIUS PICCOLOMINI (1405–1464) Piccolomini was born into a poor but noble family near Siena, Italy. He studied law in Siena and worked for many years as a secretary for cardinals and bishops. Piccolomini became known for his writings, which included poems, a novel, a comic play, and essays on church issues. In the 1440s, he became a priest and was later named bishop of Siena. In the fall of 1454, as Pope Nicholas V's representative, Piccolomini attended an imperial assembly in Frankfurt, where he saw quires of Gutenberg's Bible. Piccolomini went on to become a cardinal. In 1458 he was named Pope Pius II.

PETER SCHÖFFER (CA. 1425–1503) Schöffer was born at Gernsheim on the Rhine, a short journey south and across the river from Mainz. He may be the Petrus Ginsheym who studied at the University of Erfurt in 1444. Otherwise, the first documentary evidence of him is an elegantly written colophon that he wrote in Paris in 1449, when he finished copying a manuscript by Aristotle. In the early 1450s, Schöffer was among the craftspeople hired to work with Gutenberg and Fust to print the 42-line Bible. Schöffer attended the fateful hearing of November 6, 1455, as a witness for Fust, and he continued to work for Fust on the magnificent Mainz Psalter and other beautifully printed books. After Fust's death, Schöffer took over the business and married Fust's daughter. He continued to specialize in luxury books—mainly psalters, missals, law books, and works of theology—and built up a successful business, which sent representatives to sell his books over a wide area, from Scandinavia to Switzerland. After Schöffer died, his son Johann carried on the business. Two other sons also became printers.

SEJONG OF KOREA (1397–1450) King Sejong was the fourth ruler of the Choson dynasty (1392–1910). Like his father, King Taejong, he encouraged printing with metal type, believing that "to govern it is necessary to spread knowledge of the laws and the books so as to satisfy reason and to reform men's evil nature; in this way peace and order may be maintained." He issued several decrees for metal type to be cast and paid for by the royal treasury. Printing, however, was limited to official government printing shops. Woodblock printing continued for works intended for wide distribution, such as calendars, almanacs, and educational books. More scholarly books were printed with movable type. During Sejong's thirty-two-year reign (1418–1450), 308 books were printed, about half of them with movable type—and all before Gutenberg's Bible.

PROCOPIUS WALDVOGEL (MID-1400S) Procopius Waldvogel was a goldsmith from Prague who, according to contracts written in 1444 and 1446, agreed to teach some citizens of Avignon, France, the art of "artificial writing." The documents mention steel alphabets (punches?), "forms" of tin (matrices?), Hebrew letters made of iron, and other vaguely described equipment of metal and wood. His pupils paid him monthly fees for their lessons, swore to keep what they learned secret, and promised not to practice their new skills within a 30-mile (48 km) radius of Avignon. No evidence survives of anything printed as a result of these lessons, and Waldvogel disappears from historic records after 1446.

SOURCE NOTES

4 Geoffrey Chaucer, "To His Scribe Adam," in *The Riverside Chaucer*, ed. Larry D. Benson, 3rd ed. (Boston: Houghton Mifflin, 1987), 650 (My translation).

19–20 James Westfall Thomson, *The Medieval Library* (Chicago: University of Chicago Press, 1939), 607.

20 *Petrarch: Four Dialogues for Scholars*, trans. C. H. Rawski (Cleveland: Press of Western Reserve University, 1967), 35.

26 Douglas C. McMurtrie, *The Gutenberg Documents* (New York: Oxford University Press, 1941), 117.

29 Albert Kapr, *Johann Gutenberg: The Man and His Invention*, trans. Douglas Martin (Aldershot, UK: Scolar Press, 1996), 65.

30 McMurtrie, 86.

33 Otto W. Fuhrmann, *Gutenberg and the Strasbourg Documents of 1439* (New York: Press of the Woolly Whale, 1940), 174.

38 McMurtrie, 109.

39 Ibid., 123.

42 Thomas Francis Carter, *The Invention of Printing in China and Its Spread Westward*, revised by L. Carrington Goodrich, 2nd ed. (New York: Ronald Press Company, 1955), 212.

44 British Library, "Diamond Sutra," *British Library Online Gallery*, n.d., http://www.bl.uk/onlinegallery/themes/landmarks/diamondsutra.htm (April 22, 2007).

48 Carter, 212.

49 Ibid., 213.

49 Ibid., 216.

49 Ibid., 227.

52 John Man, *Gutenberg: How One Man Remade the World with Words* (New York: John Wiley, 2002), 113.

59 Kapr, 106.

62 Martin Davies, *The Gutenberg Bible* (London: British Library, 1996), 20.

70 Kapr, 212.

81 Ibid., 170.

81 Davies, 20.

84 McMurtie, 186.

88 Theodore L. De Vinne, *The Invention of Printing* (New York: Francis Hart & Co., 1876), 465.

99 Stephan Füssel, *Gutenberg and the Impact of Printing,* trans. Douglas Martin (Aldershot, UK: Ashgate Publishing Co., 2005), 51.

102 Kapr, 259.

102 Ibid.

103 Ibid.

104 Ibid., 264.

104 McMurtrie, 219.

106 Elizabeth L. Eisenstein, *The Printing Revolution in Early Modern Europe,* 2nd ed. (Cambridge: Cambridge University Press, 2005), 13.

109 Ibid., 347.

109 Man, 228.

113 Eisenstein, 39.

114 Füssel, *Gutenberg and the Impact of Printing,* 110.

121 Man, 27.

121 Stephan Füssel, *Johannes Gutenberg* (Reinbek bei Hamburg: Rowolt Taschenbuch Verlag, 1999), 7 (My translation).

122 Füssel, *Johannes Gutenberg,* 141 (My translation).

122 Victor Hugo, *Notre-Dame de Paris,* 1831 (Literature Network), bk. 5, chap. 2, 2000, http://www.online -literature.com/victor _hugo/hunchback_notre _dame/24/ (August 13, 2007).

122 Mark Twain, "Directory of Mark Twain's Maxims, Quotations, and Various Opinions," *Twainquotes.com,* n.d., http://www.twainquotes .com/Gutenberg.html (November 11, 2006).

124 Mary Bellis, "Inventors of the Modern Computer," *About.com,* 2007, http://inventors.about .com/library/weekly/ aa091598.htm (April 2, 2007).

125 James Thorpe, *The Gutenberg Bible: Landmark in Learning* (San Marino, CA: Huntington Library, 1999), 30.

129 McMurtrie, 72.

129 For examples, see McMurtrie, 81, 88.

144 DeVinne, 465.

145 Füssel, *Johannes Gutenberg*, 94–95 (My translation).

147 Lucien Febvre and Henri-Jean Martin, *The Coming of the Book: The Impact of Printing 1450–1800*, trans. David Gerard (London: Verso, 1997), 76.

147 Kapr, 106.

SELECTED BIBLIOGRAPHY

PRIMARY SOURCES:

Biblia Latina. Mainz, GER: Johannes Gutenberg and Associates, CA. 1454.

Fuhrmann, Otto W. *Gutenberg and the Strasbourg Documents of 1439.* New York: Press of the Woolly Whale, 1940.

McMurtrie, Douglas C. *The Gutenberg Documents.* New York: Oxford University Press, 1941.

SECONDARY SOURCES:

Arens, Fritz. *Das Goldene Mainz.* Mainz, GER: Matthias-Grünewald Verlag, 1952.

Avrin, Leila. *Scribes, Script and Books: The Book Arts from Antiquity to the Renaissance.* Chicago: American Library Association, 1991.

Bühler, Curt F. *The Fifteenth-Century Book.* Philadelphia: University of Pennsylvania Press, 1960.

Carter, Thomas Francis. *The Invention of Printing in China and Its Spread Westward.* 2nd ed. Revised by L. Carington Goodrich. New York: The Ronald Press, 1955.

Chappell, Warren, and Robert Bringhurst. *A Short History of the Printed Word.* 2nd ed. Revised by Point Roberts. Washington, DC: Hartley & Marks, 1999.

Davies, Martin. *The Gutenberg Bible.* London: The British Library, 1996.

DeVinne, Theodore L. *The Invention of Printing.* 1876. Reprint, Detroit: Gale Research Company, 1969.

Eisenstein, Elizabeth L. *The Printing Revolution in Early Modern Europe.* 2nd ed. Cambridge: Cambridge University Press, 2005.

Enste, Norbert. *Gutenberg in Eltville, or How the Printed Word Took over the World.* Translated by Geraldine Blecker. In Exhibition Catalog. Eltville, GER: Town Council of Eltville, 2000.

Febvre, Lucien, and Henri-Jean Martin. *The Coming of the Book: The Impact of Printing 1450–1800*. Translated by David Gerard. London: Verso, 1997.

Freeman, Janet Ing. *Johann Gutenberg and His Bible*. New York: Typophiles, 1988.

Füssel, Stephan. *Gutenberg and the Impact of Printing*. Translated by Douglas Martin. Aldershot, UK: Ashgate Publishing, 2005.

———. *Johannes Gutenberg*. Reinbek bei Hamburg: Rowolt Taschenbuch Verlag, 1999.

Geck, Elisabeth. *Johannes Gutenberg, from Lead Letter to the Computer*. Bad Godesberg, GER: Inter Nationes, 1968.

Goff, Frederick R. *The Permanence of Johann Gutenberg*. Austin: Humanities Research Center at the University of Texas, 1970.

Jensen, Kristin, ed. *Incunabula and their Readers: Printing, Selling, and Using Books in the Fifteenth Century*. London: British Library, 2003.

Kapr, Albert. *Johann Gutenberg: The Man and His Invention*. Translated by Douglas Martin. Aldershot, UK: Scolar Press, 1996.

Kilgour, Frederick G. *The Evolution of the Book*. New York: Oxford University Press, 1998.

Köster, Kurt. *Gutenberg in Strassburg*. Mainz, GER: Gutenberg-Gesellschaft, 1973.

Man, John. *Gutenberg: How One Man Remade the World with Words*. New York: John Wiley, 2002.

McMurtrie, Douglas C. *Some Facts Concerning the Invention of Printing*. Chicago: Chicago Club of Printing House Craftsmen, 1939.

Needham, Paul. "The Text of the Gutenberg Bible." In *Trasmisssione dei Testi a Stampa nel Periodo Moderno* 2: 43–84. Rome: Edizione dell'Ateneo, 1985.

———. "Paleography and the Earliest Printing Types." In *Johannes Gutenberg—Regionale Aspekte des frühen Buchdrucks*. Berlin: Staatsbibliothek zu Berlin, 1993.

Nicholas, David. *The Transformation of Europe 1300–1600*. New York: Oxford University Press, 1999.

Pick, Erhart. *Münzen, Mächte und Mäzene: 2000 Jahre Geld in Stadt und Kurstaat Mainz*. Mainz, GER: Verlag Philipp von Zabern, 2006.

Pierpont Morgan Library. *The Fifteenth-Century Book, An Exhibition Arranged for the 500th Anniversary of the Invention of Printing*. Introduction by Lawrence C. Wroth. New York: Pierpont Morgan Library, 1940.

Ruppel, Aloys. *Johannes Gutenberg, Sein Leben und Sein Werk*. 3rd ed. Nieuwkoop, NETH: B. de Graaf, 1967.

Scholderer, Victor. *Johann Gutenberg, The Inventor of Printing*. London: Trustees of the British Museum, 1963.

Schwab, R. N. "Cyclotron Analyses of the Ink in the 42-Line Bible." *Papers of the Bibliographical Society of America* 77 (1983): 285–315.

Steinberg, S. H. *Five Hundred Years of Printing*. Revised by John Trevitt. London: British Library, 1996.

Stillwell, Margaret Bingham. *The Beginning of the World of Books, 1450 to 1470*. New York: Bibliographical Society of America, 1972.

Thomson, James Westfall. *The Medieval Library*. Chicago: University of Chicago Press, 1939.

Thorpe, James. *The Gutenberg Bible: Landmark in Learning*. San Marino, CA: Huntington Library, 1999.

Winship, George Parker. *Printing in the Fifteenth Century*. Philadelphia: University of Pennsylvania Press, 1940.

FURTHER READING AND WEBSITES

BOOKS

Beller, Susan Provost. *The History Puzzle: How We Know What We Know about the Past.* Minneapolis: Twenty-First Century Books, 2006.

Brookfield, Karen. *Book.* New York: Alfred A. Knopf, 1993.

Day, Nancy. *Your Travel Guide to Renaissance Europe.* Minneapolis: Twenty-First Century Books, 2001.

Heinrichs, Ann. *The Printing Press.* New York: Franklin Watts, 2005.

McMurtrie, Douglas C. *Wings for Words.* New York: Rand McNally, 1940.

Needham, Paul, ed. "Johann Gutenberg and Printing." *Calliope* 13, no. 6 (February, 2003).

Pollard, Michael. *Johann Gutenberg, Master of Modern Printing.* Woodbridge, CT: Blackbirch Press, 2001.

Rees, Fran. *Johannes Gutenberg, Inventor of the Printing Press.* Minneapolis: Compass Point Books, 2006.

Zuehlke, Jeffrey. *Germany in Pictures.* Minneapolis: Twenty-First Century Books, 2003.

WEBSITES

The First Four Printed Bibles in the Scheide Library
http://www.princeton.edu/~rbsc/exhibitions/scheide/scheide_bibles.pdf
This Princeton University website presents illustrations and information about the Gutenberg Bible, Mentelin's Bible, the 36-line Bible, and Fust and Schöffer's 1462 Bible.

The Gutenberg Bible at the Ransom Center
http://www.hrc.utexas.edu/exhibitions/permanent/gutenberg/
This site from the University of Texas at Austin provides information about Gutenberg, the Bible, and digital images of the Ransom Center copy.

Gutenberg Digital
http://www.gutenbergdigital.de/gudi/eframes/index.htm
Digital images of every page of the Gutenberg Bible at Göttingen
University in Germany are available on this site. It also offers information and images of other documents concerning Gutenberg and
the history of printing.

The Gutenberg Homepage
http://www.mainz.de/Gutenberg/English/index.htm
This site includes information on "The Time of Gutenberg,"
"Gutenberg and Mainz," and "The Gutenberg Bible."

The Keio Gutenberg Bible
http://www.humi.keio.ac.jp/treasures/incunabula/B42-web/b42/html/
index01.html
Digital images of every page of the Gutenberg Bible at Keio
University in Japan are available on this site.

Landmarks in Printing
http://www.bl.uk/onlinegallery/themes/landmarksprint.html
The British Library's Online Gallery has images and information
about the *Diamond Sutra* and Korean printing from metal type before
Gutenberg.

Treasures in Full: The Gutenberg Bible
http://www.bl.uk/treasures/gutenberg/homepage.html
Digital images of both of the British Library copies of the Gutenberg
Bible as well as detailed information about Gutenberg and printing
are available on this site.

INDEX

ABOUT THE AUTHOR

Diana Childress is the author of six nonfiction books and biographies for young people. Always fascinated by medieval stories, her interest in the Middle Ages grew when she studied in Germany on a Fulbright scholarship. She later returned to the United States to do graduate work in medieval English literature. She lives in New York City, the current home of four of the Bibles Gutenberg printed, one of which, on display at the New York Public Library, was a daily inspiration as she researched Gutenberg and the invention of printing.

PHOTO ACKNOWLEDGMENTS